500 DATES.....

And Still

No Happy Ending

The Good, The Bad, & The Ugly of Online Dating

DONALD GORBACH

Illustrations by Dave Wilson
Cover Design by David Creps

To Carlyn — If only I met you in my travels, I would never have had 500.

Copyright © 2015 Donald Gorbach
All rights reserved.

ISBN: 1502910667
ISBN 13: 9781502910660

www.500-dates.com

DON'T HAVE TIME FOR YOUR BULLSHIT

I don't like lairs(sic), pompous jerks, am not attracted to obesity, unrefined men or people with bad: shoes, clothes, hairs, aspirations, grammar....if you should come with an urban dictionary, I'm mostly not interested. Do not like it when a man cannot keep my mind mentality(sic) peaked towards him or does not acknowledge me with eye contact when I'm speaking to him. I do not like it when a man neglects to manscape. I'm not talking about untrimmed beards/eyebrows, nose hair, head hair....I do not like BO at all. I've been known to douse people with my perfume.

<u>(actual profile taken directly from most popular online dating site)</u>

A SEXY LETTER TO THE AUTHOR

"I don't know you but I get these butterflies in my stomach every time I read your profile and stare at your beautiful photos. My God. I have to send your folks a bottle of wine for their fine creation...Michelangelo, Sistine Chapel doesn't outbid your parents creation....then I read on, and you spark flames out of my blood....You see it starts with a rush, then gets defined and sharpens into lust...I have such neediness to fall into a man's touch, just let myself go, be lead by a sexual animal who is in much heat as I am, trust in his creativity to do what pleases his hard member, teasing me to pieces while search for the spots that make me growl and moan, me following your silent demands that you make on my body....You are like an aphrodisiac so intoxicating, and everywhere you touch...you leave trails of fire behind. This is power, this is passion, this is defining me!! I crave you like a drug...you and I will experience volumes...the beginning of a trilogy, the beginning of an epic. I am so passionate about long steamy deep tonguing each others mouth...your lips will be treated like the finest truffles; savored slowly, delectable, till my gums hurt from your flavor! I trust you...there is no other man that has excited me this much ever. You fulfill me. You have no equal. I am not the same anymore...damaged goods...you have successfully captured my interest...by entire being by a frisson of hot blooded thrill...so maybe I don't know of you. Is this high risk? High risk, high return right? You complete my image. No worries on losing me. I am drawn to your imagination, creativity, innovative thinking, willing contribution, execution excellence in your choice of words...I am surrendering my lust to you. I like the sappy side of you....I like everything....I feel safe already, and one thing I'd like promise you is that I will never take you for granted. You will always feel wanted, desired, needed and appreciated for all that you are. Nothing could keep me away….I'm yours."

Dedication

It was long before the invention of personal computers and internet dating when my Mom and Dad met. As a matter of fact it was so long ago, I've insisted it was possibly even before Thomas Edison came up with the idea for electricity. My folks disagree, of course, chiding that I'm a little off on the historic timeline of the two events.

Nevertheless, their meeting occurred on a little beach in Bridgeport, Connecticut one sunny afternoon and Dad knew instantly he wanted this woman to be his wife. Not much for procrastination, Dad quickly secured a date with her. It was on their third get-together that Dad proposed. Mom's response was, "Marry you? I'm not sure I even want to go out with you again!" In today's world, Dad would have been deleted from Mom's contact list after the first date.

Mom and Dad's meeting was what you might call "conventional." Today, internet dating has become the mainstream methodology for social connection and has morphed the whole idea of "conventional" meeting into a new era. Younger generations of mate-seekers are exploring well beyond their local beaches via the internet in the hopes of finding love and companionship. The momentum of this social change has grown bigger than a tidal wave, bringing with it the most diverse and interesting of human interaction. That is what this book is about.

Whether it was Dad's determination or providence in action, he presented the ring and a wedding date was set. I'm happy to say, they just celebrated their Sixty First Anniversary.

For Generation X, Y and Z, let this be proof-certain that finding a life companion is possible – whether it is by old fashion convention or internet determination!

To Mom and Dad I dedicate this book. May their long and devoted life together serve as an inspiration to all who are vigilant in their quest for a mate.

TABLE OF CONTENTS

Dedication vii
Introduction 1

"THE UGLY"
Match.com's Worst Nightmare Ever 8
Match.com's $10,000,000 Lawsuit. 11
Google Executive Made Bad Arrangement. 13
A Craigslist Killer's Survivor 15
Plenty of Fish's Blackmailer 17
The Absent-Minded Professor 20
Natalie's Nightmare 24
The Black Widow 28
The Internet Casanova 30
Paranoia 32
Not So Sweet Caroline 35
To Russia With Love 40

"THE BAD"
I've Been Hacked 44
What's Your Husband Doing Here? 47
Husband Has Anger Issues 51
Grossly Misrepresented 54
Butter Face 57
Yoga Bear 60
Call Me Maybe? 62
That's My Baby 65
Brother Can You Spare A Dime? 69
I'm Mad As Hell And I'm Not Going To Take It Anymore . . 71
Once A Cheater 74
Till Death Do Us Part 76
AOL: Always On Line 80

Do You Take Checks? 84
Payback Is A Bitch 88
Home Shopping 91
Tony or Tonya? 97
Who Let The Dog Out 100
No Class In First Class 103
Sight For Sore Eyes 106
Cruise To Nowhere Nightmare 109
Dirty Girl 114
Diaper Dan 118
On Pins And Needles 121
Coming Into The Closet 123
Deal Killers 125
We'll Take The Double-D's Please 128
Two Hours Equals Two Years 132
My Date With A Bank Robber 135
Dating Myself 138
Five Drink Rule 141
What Kind of Car Do You Drive? 144
Bats All Folks! 147
My $1200 Dinner Date 150
All She Could Eat 153
Pizza Disaster 156
Food Fight 161
Texting While Dining 164
Family Ties 166
Your Kitchen Is On Fire 170

"THE GOOD WITH THE BAD"
Something For Everyone 174
Female Supremacy 176
My Daddy, My Pimp 179
Will Work For Boobs 183
Lactate Tolerance 185

A Strange Profession 187
Fit To Be Tied 190
His Sexy Beard 193
Like A Good Neighbor 196
All Choked Up 199
The Fake Internet Girlfriend Service. 201
Professional Daters 203
Beware of Separate Bedrooms 206
Beware of Separate Bathrooms. 209
The Girl With Too Much Baggage. 211
The Girl With Not Enough Baggage 214
Little Italy…Little In Common 216
Menu Flambé 219
My Bloody Valentine 221
I Think I Killed Your Dog. 226
Drive By. 230
Identity Theft 232
Kelly Girl. 235
A Real Conundrum 238
The $5,000 Perfect Girlfriend. 240

"THE GOOD"
A Friend With Benefits 244
Too Good To Be True! 246
Naughty But Nice. 249
The Office Perk 251
Money Can Buy Happiness. 255
Buy My Boobs And I'm Yours Forever 258
Three's Company 261
A Real Trifecta 263
Room With A View 265
She Blew My Mind. 268
Twisted Sisters 271
Winning 274

Rules Are Meant To Be Broken 277
More Than A Grand Slam 280
I Dream Of Jenny................................ 283
Kate Upton, Will You Go To The Prom With Me? 285
Celebrity Online Daters 287
Think You're Too Good For Online Dating? 289
Lobster Love 291
Take Me Out With The Crowd..................... 294
A Real Catch.................................... 298
Pretty Woman 301
Don't Marry For Money 305
Here's To You Mrs. Robinson...................... 307
A Match Made In Heaven......................... 310

Epilogue... 312
Author's Story.. 314

INTRODUCTION

And So The Journey Begins

I went on a date the other night and met a gorgeous young lady who was waiting for me at the bar. She looked exactly like her profile picture. She appeared to be thirty-something with a magnificent face and an outfit that highlighted every curve of her amazing body. We exchanged a few introductory comments, and then proceeded outside to a waterfront area where we were seated at our table. We ordered an appetizer, crab and artichoke dip, and a couple glasses of wine. We were relaxed, feeling quite comfortable with each other. The chemistry seemed strong. What could possibly go wrong with this romantic dinner and my more than-striking woman? The answer would come soon enough.

Finishing with the small talk, I proceeded to tell this lovely woman that I am an author. "Actually," I said, "I'm writing a book about internet dating stories."

"Oh," she says and then hesitates before asking, "What kind of stories?"

I explain that I am looking for great dating stories and she asks, "Is that why you are online?

Before I could complete the word "partially" in answering her question, she stood up and poured her glass of chardonnay on my shoulder, then told me I was an a-hole and thanked me for wasting her time as she towered over me like a fire-breathing dragon.

I was startled to say the least. My brain couldn't compute what had just happened and I quickly got up, following her as she mainlined toward the front entrance. "What are you talking about," I asked innocently enough? I begged.

"If I had known you brought me here to interrogate me about dating stories, I would have never accepted the date."

"That wasn't my only intention, "I sincerely pleaded. "I really am looking for love."

She was steadfast in her anger and told me to quit the bullshitting like all the others. My reply slipped right out, "You mean you've dated other authors?" I was trying to be funny to lighten the heat. It didn't help.

Normally, an incident like this would be quite upsetting to me, especially in a public place. Being doused by a good glass of chardonnay hardly put me in the greatest spotlight. And just when my date slammed the door in my face, a witty waitress appeared behind me asking, "Can I get you another glass of wine?" We both broke out in hysterics.

I retrieved my car from the valet and headed for home feeling ambivalent over the evening's outcome and my sports coat now stained with chardonnay. I consoled myself with the idea it was just another day at work.

This story is significant as it really lays the perfect foundation for this book and internet dating in general. Although most members on dating sites aren't writing a book or deceiving their dates by pretending to be looking for the perfect mate, they are lying nevertheless. Okay, maybe lying is too strong of a word to use, but deceiving, concealing, embellishing or misrepresentation certainly fits.

After dating more than 500 women, using 8 online sites, and spending over $200,000 on dinners, trips, upfront dates and special arrangements, I have found five common areas of dishonesty that are prevalent. In all cases, the deceptions are committed as if they are acceptable protocols in the world of dating. Nicely put, these "misrepresentations" are: Age, Income, Marital Status, Weight or Body Type, and more disappointing than cold soup at dinner, are the solely outdated profile pictures. Whether these pictures were high school photos, engagement photos, "before/after" photos, pictures that were taken immediately after application of Rogaine, hair plugs, hair color applications, hair extensions, etc., it doesn't matter. Thanks to the invention of photo shop, they are all very deceiving. So for my first date who called me a liar for deceiving her with my misguided intentions, it is obvious that my non-disclosure was not a serious infraction compared to most. That's how I like to justify it!

And speaking of disclosure, although many of these stories were my own personal experiences, there are those that were given to me by friends, colleagues, newspaper items and yes, from actual dates solicited by me over dinner. In fact, my opening line on many dates was, "have you had any interesting dating stories on this site so far"? Many of their stories are contained within.

The subtitle of this book, *The Good, the Bad, and the Ugly* does not pertain to the physical characteristics of women, or lack thereof. Instead, it's actually the way I have decided to categorize my stories. One section of the book, not named in the title, is called *The Good With The Bad*. These are stories that some people may view as bad dates, and others may view as "not so terrible." I like to think they were lemons served to me, and I was able to make lemonade with them. You decide if you think I was successful. The *Ugly* stories speak for themselves. They have elements of violence, deceit, illegal activities, assaults, and even murders. Many of these stories are disturbing and shocking. I included a minimal amount of these tales only because I felt that they needed to be told. They serve as a warning to others as to what could and has happened on dates with strangers online. These stories are deliberately located in the beginning of the book, because my intent was to make the book as light and entertaining as possible. In other words, I didn't want to save them for the end, and leave you with either a jaded opinion of online dating or worse, horrible nightmares.

With regards to names and identities of actual dates throughout the book, names and places have been changed to protect the innocent, and to assure my dates that their secrets would remain safe with me. And yes, speaking of my dates, I learned a very valuable lesson after my first one. I never started the conversation again with "oh by the way, I'm writing a dating storybook." It wasn't that I didn't want to be honest with them. I tried that route before. I just didn't want another wine bath and another embarrassing and humiliating scene in a public place. Been there, done that.

And speaking of embarrassing scenes, bizarre moments and incredible women for the most part, my goal was to keep this book to 101 greatest stories, especially after 500 dates. I actually had another 100 stories that I could have included. But, for the sake of keeping your interest, and maybe continuing this series for later, I picked out my favorites. I hope you enjoy reading about these experiences as much as I enjoyed bringing them to you. It was a lot of hard work, time, money and yes, even sex involved, but I did it all for you. To inspire, teach and yes, even warn against potential dangers. I hope you enjoy reading it as much as I've enjoyed bringing my reality to you.

"The Ugly"

Match.com's Worst Nightmare Ever

Imagine being a woman and answering a profile of a handsome young man who stated that his profession was a surgeon. You would think that it was your lucky day and that you might have found the man of your dreams. You end up messaging him, and you actually end up meeting him for dinner one night. He is charming. He tells you many stories that in his young life, he's had unbelievable jobs including being an astronaut with NASA and even worked as a CIA. After dinner, he might invite you back to his place, where you have a glass of wine or two, and then that's the last thing you remember about the evening. You wake up the next morning in the doctor's bed, without your clothes on, nauseous, and having no recollection of anything that happened the evening before.

Well, welcome to the nightmare which happened to 21 women in Philadelphia. All these women went through a similar scenario with the same man, Jeffrey Marsalis, aka Dr. Jeff. None of these women knew each other, but yet they all had the same date with the doctor, which involved a bar, a blackout, and a confusing morning. The conclusion, they had all been drugged and raped.

The most amazing thing about these women is that they did not go to the police right away. They did not know that a crime took place. They rationalized that they just got drunk, and had sex with the doctor, and they had no idea that they had actually been drugged and raped. They remembered nothing. In fact, the most incredible thing was that many of them continued dating the doctor. He was charming, witty and treated them very well. They actually continued having consensual sex with the doctor, because after all, they had already given themselves to the doctor, so there was no reason not to continue. He made them feel wanted and needed.

It wasn't until police began investigating one of Marsalis' ex girlfriends, who reported being date raped, that all the women came forward with the same stories. Ten of these cases were prosecuted, but unbelievably, Dr. Jeff was acquitted of these rape charges. The main reason why was because none of them went to the police right away, so there was no proof of foul play, and no evidence of them ever being drugged. Thus, no evidence that their sex wasn't consensual.

Finally, the good doctor made a major mistake He again went out on the prowl with another woman, this time in Idaho. The difference, in this case, was that the woman he drugged and raped knew she had been raped, and she went to the police immediately and was processed by a "rape kit". The prosecution was able to make this case stick, because unlike the other women, there was no way that this victim would have given her consent to a sexual act to the good doctor. She was a lesbian.

This time, a jury found Marsalis guilty of rape. Since his history of similar acts in Philadelphia came out at his sentencing, he was given a life sentence. Marsalis is believe to be the worst online date rapist in history.

Take-Away: A person has to be so careful today dating online. You don't know the history or the character of the person. You

don't know what information is true on their profile. Not everyone has true intentions. Don't take anything for granted. Don't assume anything. Proceed cautiously and slowly. Meet in a public place, tell your friends where you're going and who you're going to be with, and never, ever, leave your drink out of your sight.

Match.com's $10,000,000 Lawsuit

Talk about stalking. A Las Vegas Real Estate Agent, Mary Kay Beckman, is suing *Match.com* for $10,000,000. Her lawsuit is the result of a brutal attack she endured at the hands of a man she met on the site. She claims that *Match.com* failed to warn her about the dangers of meeting "an individual whose intentions are not to find a mate."

According to her complaint, Ms. Beckman met a guy named Wade Ridley in September 2010. They dated for approximately ten days before Mary Kay decided she didn't want to continue their romance. That's when Ridley began sending her threatening and harassing messages. On January 21, 2011, Ridley attacked Beckman in the garage at her home. He stabbed her multiple times with a butcher knife and when the knife broke, he stomped on her head and left her for dead. He later confessed that he did not intend to hurt her, but rather to kill her.

Beckman fortunately survived the brutal attack, and after two years of multiple surgeries and months of hospitalizations she lives to tell her story and speak out against online dating. Her suit against *Match*.com accuses the company of "negligence, negligent misrepresentation, deceptive trade, failure to warn and negligent infliction of emotional distress". In a statement to NBC News, *Match*.com said that what happened to Beckman "is horrible, but this lawsuit is absurd. The many millions of people who have found love on *Match*.com and other online dating sites know how fulfilling it is. And while that doesn't make what happened in this case any less awful, this is about a sick, twisted individual with no prior criminal record, not an entire community of men and women looking to meet each other."

While Beckman was still in the hospital, Ridley met another woman on *Match.com* from Arizona. Only a few weeks after he had attacked Beckman, the Arizona woman was found murdered. Ridley was charged. He ultimately killed himself while in jail before he could be tried for the murder. He was a man who turned violent.

Since these attacks, *Match.com* and two other dating sites, eHarmony and Spark Networks, have signed a joint statement of business principals agreeing to screen for sex offenders. However, even if this safeguard had been in place before September 2010, Ridley would not have been flagged.

Google Executive Made Bad Arrangement

When businessman Forest Timothy Hayes, a married father of five, contacted online dating site *Seeking Arrangement*, he had no idea that the woman he met would one day be accused of murdering him aboard his yacht. It seems that Hayes had an arrangement with a woman named Alix Catherine Tichelman; whereas, Hayes was paying Tichelman an allowance of between $3,000 and $5,000 a month for companionship. The site, bills itself as "the leading Sugar Daddy dating site," where over 3 million members seek mutually beneficial relationships. The site insists that it's not promoting prostitution, even though Tichelman boasted on her profile that she had over 200 clients. It's simply a site where women "are looking for men who can provide financial assistance for them", said Angela Jacob Bermudo with Seeking Arrangement.

Call it what you wish, Hayes met Tichelman on the site and security footage aboard his yacht shows that Tichelman not only administered a lethal heroin injection to her "sugar daddy", but instead of calling 911 when Hayes slipped into unconsciousness, she did just the opposite. Video shows that she proceeded to gather up her drugs, and not only walks over Hayes' dying body several times, but she continues to drink her wine. And if that wasn't heartless and "cold" in itself, Tichelman doesn't leave the boat until she conceals the dead body.

I guess it's safe to say that not all arrangements end badly. But this wasn't the first suspicious death that Tichelman was involved in. She was a suspect in the death of another "boyfriend" months prior to Hayes.

Take-Away: What seems to be the common denominator on most of these dating sites is that there are no background checks and balances required. It is definitely a business of numbers, and until more precautions are taken by these large companies, more tragedies and illegal activities will continue to occur.

A Craigslist Killer's Survivor

Remember the name Ted Bundy? He was an American serial killer, rapist, kidnapper and necrophiliac who murdered numerous young women and girls in the 1970's. He was ultimately apprehended and confessed to thirty or more homicides. All this happened before the World Wide Web was available to everyday people. I bring this cold blooded killer's story to light for a reason.

Bundy was regarded as handsome and charismatic by his young female victims, traits he exploited in winning their trust. He typically approached these women and girls in public places, feigning an injury or disability or impersonating an authority figure before overpowering and assaulting them at some secluded location.

Moving the clock ahead forty years with the power of the internet at his disposal, imagine how much easier Bundy's criminal and murderous activities would have been. He likely would have committed even more murders.

Philip Markoff, known as the *Craigslist* Killer, was also a handsome and charismatic guy. He was a smart medical student who attended Boston University. He was engaged to a beautiful woman and set to be married within a year of his first tirade that involved a woman named Trisha Leffler. Trisha was a masseuse who placed an ad on *Craigslist* offering her services. She advertised that she was searching for guys who wanted relief from an experienced Las Vegas girl. Markoff answered the ad. They met in the lobby of the Westin Hotel where Trisha interviewed her prospective client before taking him to her room for the massage. She felt comfortable with him and described him as a "tall, good looking guy…He was just someone who I thought I could trust. Just a regular looking guy."

However, this regular looking guy wasn't so regular. The moment he was alone with Leffler in her room, he commenced to tie her up, rob her at gunpoint and only because she offered no resistance, he left her unharmed. But it was only days later that Markoff found Julissa Brisman, another woman on *Craigslist*, and murdered her in cold blood. Fortunately, he was identified immediately by his robbery victim and while awaiting his trial for murder, Markoff committed suicide in his jail cell.

Markoff was apparently able to keep his double life hidden from his family, friends and even his fiancé for a long time. Despite his outstanding academic standing and seemingly normal appearance, he had dark secrets. Unbeknownst to others, it was also later discovered that he had been frequenting online sites that specialized in alternative sex, bondage and sadomasochism. He was a person you'd never have suspected of harboring such bizarre fetish attractions much less someone inclined to committing murder.

Take-Away: Criminal experts tell us these (good looking educated) are the kind of people who are most dangerous. They're the ones you least expect to commit some heinous crime. They are the ones who will get you when your guard is down.

Plenty of Fish's Blackmailer

This is a true story I recently uncovered that should serve as a warning to anyone who does online dating.

Robert Li was a 33 year old man from Winnipeg who had been laid off from his job and living in the basement of his parents' home. Maybe he was depressed, lonely and generally feeling like a loser. Maybe since he had no income and too much spare time on his hands, he lost his balance and temporarily fell off the edge of good judgment. But as the story was reported, this man with no prior criminal record devised a scheme to blackmail two different women he met on an online dating website. His intent was to swindle them out of thousands of dollars.

It happens that both women were school teachers in England, but had no connection to each other except that Li was successful in using the same con game on both of them. Once the police became involved, the two separate incidents were linked together.

Li had gone on the *Plenty of Fish* website and created a dramatic story to reel in the sympathies and love of gullible women and hook them on his line. He found two and courted both ladies over a period of time via chat line and Skype under the guise of being a trustworthy man, but all the while using a bogus last name and building his romantic web of deception. According to Li's elaborate tale, he was in the process of moving to London where both his intended victims of the blackmail scheme resided. He told them that his father was deep in debt to an Asian gang who were after him to pay up.

Eventually Li talked a convincing enough story to persuade one of the smitten women into performing a striptease for him while on Skype. Little did she know he was videoing the whole thing to use against her. Once he manipulated the online relationship to that level of intimacy, he then told her he would be traveling to London in the coming days to be with her. She was a lady-in-waiting and anxious to consummate their relationship. His trip to London, of course, never happened because he claimed he had been attacked by the Asian gang his father was in debt to. His passport stolen and worse yet, threatened that there would be more bloodshed if the debt was not paid quickly. That's when Li pulled the blackmail knife on her. He threatened to send the sexual video to her school and circulate it publicly if she didn't come up with the cash he needed. He gave her an hour to make up her mind.

His con with the other teacher went the same way, but he had videos and nude photos of her to use as leverage for his demand. He threatened to go online and destroy her teaching career by exposing the lewd materials to her faculty and colleagues.

Both of the terrified women went to the police rather than give in to the extortion. Li was arrested and convicted of extortion by libel, but bailed out with conditions that he have no contact with the victims, avoid dating websites and not use Skype. To date there have been no breaches of his bail so far as anyone knows.

Ladies, he's still out there!

Take-Away: Do not send revealing photos, videos, or start sexting to people you don't really know. They may use these against you at some point when you least expect it and become your worst nightmare.

The Absent-Minded Professor

You all may remember the Manti Te'o story. He was a famous Notre Dame linebacker who developed an online relationship with a girl who died before they had the opportunity to meet in person. Her death then publicly became his inspiration during a Heisman-caliber football season, but it turned out that both the girl and her death were a fiction. He had been duped by an online hoax that was perpetrated by a former high school quarterback from California.

When Manti's story became headline sports news, we all thought nobody could have really been that stupid. But it turns out many people are when caught up in online love. What happened to a

The Absent-Minded Professor

theoretical particle physicist named Paul Frampton proves the point as an even worse case of "online stupid." Frampton's story culminated for him in life changing consequences of a very negative sort!

In 2011 Paul Frampton was a 68 year old recently divorced man who was lonely and looking for love. Though still financially strapped due to his divorce, he signed up on an online dating site and began communicating with a woman he believed to be the famous Czechoslovakian bikini model Denise Milani. He became fantastically obsessed with her. She was more than beautiful with a curvaceous body to die for, a woman he would never have had a chance for in his own backyard. The glamour photos on her site displayed the gorgeous, dark-haired model as tauntingly sexy with a warm and innocent smile. But beyond all of that, Frampton's ongoing chats with her via internet drew him to her even more so. She told him how she dreamed of settling down and having a family, being exhausted from the pressures of a high profile modeling career that had already provided her with fame and fortune. She confided in him a desire to end her career, filled with ogling men, but worried that Paul might never be proud of her for having showcased herself publicly as a bikini model. Her innocent sincerity was more than Paul's manly instincts could resist. He was hooked.

By January 2012 Paul was intent on seeing Milani in person and taking her as his bride, in spite of the fact that they had yet never spoken by telephone. Milani sent him an e-ticket to meet her in Bolivia by way of Toronto and Santiago, Chile. Arriving in Toronto, he discovered that the e-ticket was not valid and after spending a full day stranded there, and three more days of travel, he finally arrived in La Paz only to find that Milani had been called away to another photo shoot in Brussels. Frampton checked into his hotel to wait for another e-ticket from her to

Brussels. However, as they were continuing to keep in constant internet contact, she then asked him if he would bring a bag she had inadvertently left behind while there. He agreed to do this and again, communicating only through the internet, they made plans to finally be united in Brussels after Paul flew there by way of Buenos Aires.

On January 20, nine days after he had begun his journey, a man arrived at Paul's hotel room with her suitcase. It was suspicious. The tattered thing was empty. Paul immediately chat lined Milani to describe what seemed to him to be an odd delivery, but she explained that the suitcase was of special sentimental importance and she felt distraught over having accidentally left it behind. With a slight sense of reservation, Paul ultimately agreed to proceed with her request to bring the suitcase and catch the last minute flight she had just arranged. He filled her empty suitcase with his dirty clothes, and dashed to the airport, checking two bags and arriving in Buenos Aires without incident where he paced the lobby all day anticipating his e-ticket on to Brussels.

The ticket arrived, and he was finally set for what he thought to be the last leg of a long, crazy journey to meet the woman of his dreams. He again checked two bags, his and hers, then counted the minutes until boarding was called for the flight to Brussels. He promptly took his place in line.

You can imagine he must have been chewing his finger nails with excitement as the line of passengers slowly began to board, but…

His name was called over the loudspeaker and quite abruptly, all his dreams of meeting Denise Milani in Brussels were over.

You guessed it. He was busted in Buenos Aires for possession of a suitcase laced with cocaine. Frampton was arrested, thrown in jail and ultimately sentenced to prison for four years and eight months, convicted of drug smuggling. The entire year-long relationship was a scam. The online con artist, pretending to be Milani, was simply engaging desperate men like Frampton to be used as drug mules. Paul Frampton is not expected to be released from the Devoto, Buenos Aires jail until the end of 2014.

Take-Away: The lesson learned here is to be very, very careful when dating online. Do not do ANYTHING for someone you have never met in person, and especially don't do anything that could possibly be illegal. If bad stuff can happen to a star linebacker and a world-renowned physicist, it could happen to just about any of us.

Natalie's Nightmare

If you're getting swept off your feet by an online date, stop! You may be getting swept into harm's way. Take the advice of someone who learned the hard way. She ignored three important safety rules for online dating that could have saved her from a very bad experience.

Rule One: Don't believe everything on profile

Rule Two: Know the warning signs.

Rule Three: Trust your gut.

In Natalie's case, the online photo of Seb made him look like he was dripping with cash when the truth behind the picture was that he had just finished a stint working on a cruise liner. His ship uniform looked aristocratic, but he was actually a second ranked surgical nurse of modest means. Endowed with classic Italian looks, the Sicilian-born man turned out to be a possessive and vengeful stalker.

Natalie had signed up on *Match.com* after a failed eight-year relationship left her no better off than middle aged and still unwed. She began looking for love, romance and marriage online. Her first several prospects led nowhere, but then she was connected with Seb who quickly charmed his way into her heart. He infatuated her with his attentiveness and humor. One month after hours of talking and swapping intimate life stories by phone, they met for lunch half way between Natalie's home and Seb's pad. Their attraction was strong and he ended up a couple days later overnight at her home.

He showered her with lavish meals and gifts over the next couple of months that they dated. However, red flags started to show up when Seb began showing bizarre possessive tendencies. He tried to impose unreasonable time restrictions on her usual activities, primarily as they involved riding and caring for her beloved horse at a nearby stable, but also on her time spent with friends. His controlling noose was tightening around her neck and their relationship turned to chaos when she wanted to end it, but Seb always found a way to win her back with apologies and promises of his undying affection.

It was only after a frightening physical altercation between them, just six months after they first met, that Natalie knew the tempestuous relationship had to end. She had nodded a greeting to a passing jogger in the park one day, which so infuriated Seb that he threw her to the ground and kicked her. She pressed assault charges, but he was able to make bail and released on the condition that he stay away from her. He didn't. That's when the stalking began.

The following week, he began harassing her with phone messages and left "I love you" notes on her car. He became compulsive in texting her phone and even disguised himself as a cleaning person to gain entrance into her apartment complex. She responded to none of it.

He then took a serious step of vengeance against her. The stable manager where she boarded Jessie, her horse, called to say the animal was seriously hurt. Her leg had been cut to the bone and the wound didn't look like an accident. Ultimately, with evidence from the stable surveillance cameras Seb was charged with the brutal attack on Natalie's horse, but it wasn't enough to prove the crime was committed by him. He was remanded into two months custody for violating the prior order to stay away from Natalie.

Just three days after he was released, Seb drove to Natalie's flat and parked outside. It was only by happenstance that Natalie is alive today as a passing police officer noticed him lurking around and investigated what looked suspicious. It was discovered that Seb had a chilling torture kit of knives, screwdrivers, scalpel blades, a tourniquet and latex gloves in his car. Most horrifying of all though, they also found syringes filled with his own blood.

Seb was arrested and found guilty, sentenced to five years in jail for injuring Natalie's horse and going equipped for burglary with the intent of inflicting grievous bodily harm. Oddly, the court dismissed the prior assault charges. During his trial though, Natalie was required to spend three emotionally grueling days on the witness stand from behind a screen testifying against him. The experience was horrendous for her, but today she is thankful for what she learned.

After the trial Natalie was fearful that Seb may have made contact with other women after his initial assault arrest and before being picked up for the second time. She checked his *Match* site only to find he had reactivated it when he was released from custody earlier. Her efforts took persistence, but she was finally able to convince *Match* to remove his profile from their site and change their monitoring to improve the safety standards for its members.

Take-Away: Natalie's story could happen to anyone. Ignoring the signs of impulsiveness, mood swings and instances of throwing money around are indications of a personality type that can lead you into a dangerous relationship, and online dating websites cannot guarantee that their users are legitimately who they present themselves to be.

The Black Widow

The black widow is a spider that is known for its venomous bite. Unlike other spiders, her web is spun in a chaotic pattern in order to catch unsuspecting prey from any direction. Once tangled in her web, the snared victim is injected with her poison and dies from either the toxic bite or because she has sucked the blood out of the paralyzed prisoner.

Melissa Ann Friedrich Weeks, age 77, has been dubbed the "Internet Black Widow" and for good reason. She has been suspected, accused and convicted of numerous crimes over the years that included murder, attempted murder, manslaughter, exploiting funds, fraud and theft. This is quite a rap sheet for a sweet little old lady, don't you think? Most of her crimes and suspected crimes were perpetrated on men that she met on internet dating sites, using certain WEB sites of choice to snare her victims.

Of her documented criminal history, you can go back to 1991 when she was convicted of manslaughter in the death of one of her two husbands. It was proved that on a deserted road she ran over the drugged man twice with her car. She told police he had raped her, but she was nevertheless sentenced after the trial to six years.

After serving only two years of that sentence, she traveled to Florida where she married a widower named Robert Friedrich.

They met at a Christian retreat. Shortly after they were wed the poor guy's health faltered and he died of cardiac arrest. No one was charged in his death, but his family believes Melissa was involved in both his illness and the sudden disappearance of his money.

Her next love affair was with a divorced man she met on *AmericanSinglesDating.com*. The day they moved in together, he was hospitalized after receiving a mysterious injury to his head. She was later charged with siphoning money from his bank account and served four years in prison for grand theft and forgery.

Apparently after getting out of the pen, she settled into a quiet life in Nova Scotia. That's when she met Fred Weeks. Fred's friend who was a justice of the peace married the couple, but soon discovered the criminal history of Fred's new wife. Fred was warned, but it was too late. While on their honeymoon he became ill and was hospitalized. Shortly thereafter, police became suspicious and Melissa was charged with attempting to poison the man. Fortunately, he didn't die.

This sweet little old lady had become good at luring grieving widowers into her web, and there's no telling how many undocumented crimes she may have committed over the years. Beware! Melissa, the Internet Black Widow, may not be the only dangerous spider on the World Wide Web of internet dating sites.

The Internet Casanova

Just imagine yourself as a twenty-seven year old guy living in the United States. You are six-foot-two with the physique and looks of Adonis, the mythological Greek god of beauty and desire. You are full of charm and wit with no responsibilities to tie you down. You have a wanderlust for life and pursue it with vigor, especially enjoying the sweet smell of romance at every opportunity. You fancy yourself to be the Most Interesting Man, but raining on your parade is one little problem, finances.

Then you discover the secret of all diabolical secrets, online dating.

Being highly intelligent, you devise a genius plot. You determine that capitalizing on your natural good looks and charm is one easy ticket to paradise, and women on the dating websites look like apples for the plucking. So you begin a jolly romp across the U.S. from the Midwest to Portland, Florida and Texas feasting on a wide variety of apple trees along the way. (Fortunately, none of them were Granny Smiths.)

This Adonis in reality is known as the Internet Casanova, aka Ray Holycross, aka Ray Parris, aka Ray Cross and aka Ray Tompson. He is now accused of defrauding some thirty-eight women that he seduced while on his travels across the country. He became quite good at using dating websites to meet women he could move in with and then steal their hearts, belongings and money. One of his ex-girlfriends discovered him to be texting thirty different women and meeting with seven to eight of them a day when he claimed to be at work.

Most of the Internet Casanova's victims truly believed he loved them before he skipped town leaving them brokenhearted. Most of them were robbed as well. But, as all good things must come to an end, the good-looking dater will be appearing in court next month in Indiana, accused of pawning an ex- girlfriend's camera. He is likewise wanted in Oregon on charges of identity theft and under active investigation for multiple other crimes. All told, thirty-eight different women across the country have come forward in an attempt to bust the Greek god's bronze statue to smithereens. He's in really big trouble now whether he realizes it or not. Looks like his jolly Casanova romp may be coming to an end.

Paranoia

First, I want to say that I've never been paranoid about anything or anyone. I normally trust people. If for some reason I get the sense that a person is not trustworthy, I simply don't have dealings with them. I just go with the idea that people are trustable unless or until they show you that they're not. It's a positive outlook.

Then I met Liza.

I found her on an online dating site called *What's Your Price*. It's a site that specializes in a pre- negotiated price for a specified date. I had negotiated to have dinner with this woman named Liza for a price of $150. She lived near one of my favorite restaurants, and we dined that evening on an outside patio overlooking a gorgeous marina. I had a pretty girl with me in a beautiful setting. What could be better?

Before our date, however, while we were negotiating the details, she suggested meeting me at a place near my home rather than at the designated restaurant. I'd never had a date ask for that arrangement much less turn it into a pushing contest with me, but I held my course and we did meet at the restaurant. Our dinner was enjoyable. We laughed and chatted, but I couldn't help notice how frequently Liza was texting on her phone. It was becoming an annoyance and rather disrespectful after the fifth or sixth time, so I finally asked if there was a problem. She told me that a girlfriend just broke up with her boyfriend. She was trying to offer advice and emotional support to her friend.

We finished our dinner and walked out of the restaurant together. I handed my valet ticket to the attendant. Liza said she hadn't used the valet, but was parked across the parking lot so I offered to walk her to her car. She politely declined my offer to escort her, then thanked me for dinner with a hug and walked away. Once my car arrived, I felt the gentlemanly thing to do was drive over to the parking lot to be sure Liza got into her vehicle safely. She had only been out of my sight for a couple minutes and when I zipped into the lot, I saw her getting into a truck. There was a man in the driver's seat. I did a u-turn and although it seemed strange that someone had picked her up, I figured it was no big deal since I wouldn't be seeing her ever again anyway.

But, it turns out I did see Liza again, in the newspaper. The story read that she had been arrested with her boyfriend for breaking into her date's home. The way the caper worked was that while Liza was on a date with a guy, the boyfriend would case the guy's home for the purpose of breaking and entering. Liza would keep her robber-boyfriend safely informed by text messaging while she dined with the unsuspecting fellow. There was speculation in the newspaper that the two of them had been successfully using that robbery plot for months, and the police were expecting to hear from more victims based on the loot that was found stashed in Liza's apartment.

I KNEW there was something a little odd about Liza from the beginning, and I suppose I should be a little paranoid more often for my own good. I'm convinced that had I met her that night near my home, I would have become one of her robbery victims too.

Take-Away: You choose the restaurant. Don't let the woman pick the first time. She may pick a very expensive one, or she might have other motives.

Not So Sweet Caroline

This is probably going to sound like the most unusual story. It's one that I haven't told anyone ever before, and I'm telling it because I think it's important that other people are aware that it can and does happen.

I met a girl a year or so ago on a very popular dating site. We met for dinner at an Italian restaurant in Boca Raton, Florida. Although my date was a little heavier, a little older and less attractive than her online picture showed her to be, I thought she dressed and presented herself well.

We ordered a round of drinks at the bar first, and right away I began thinking she seemed very aggressive. She wanted to know what I was looking for in a woman. She asked whether she was it, and I told her it was hard to tell since we had just met. In my private thoughts though I was getting an inkling that she was off a click and seemed both pushy and needy. I was quickly surmising that I didn't want to sit for hours and chat with her over dinner, so I suggested we order appetizers and stay at the bar. I sensed a glimmer of disappointment in her, but she went along with the idea. We ordered some calamari and eggplant with another round of drinks, then a third round as we continued small talk. I learned from the conversation that Caroline was from the State of Washington. This left a question mark in my mind because her profile said she was from Boca. She went on to say she was in Boca visiting friends and studying to be a nurse.

We had been there for about two hours by now and finished our fourth round of drinks. I was feeling a little buzzed, which made Caroline begin to look a little prettier to me. Call it cliché if you like, but in my thoughts I decided to change her appeal ranking from a five to a seven, but mind you seven is still not high enough for me to go for more than a first date.

Caroline went on to say she was staying at a local hotel and had taken a cab over to the restaurant. She asked if I would drive her back to her place. I asked why she was staying at a hotel if she was here visiting with friends and she explained she preferred staying in her own place. She liked her privacy. That didn't make sense to me, but who was I to judge. "Sure, I'll give you a ride to your hotel." So I summoned my car from the valet and drove to her hotel that was just a couple miles away.

When we pulled into the parking lot, Caroline insisted that it was still early. It was 10:30. She told me to come in for a drink. I thanked her of course, but said I couldn't. I said I had several appointments the next day and really should get home. "Just come in for one. Just one?"

She was persistent and I finally acquiesced under the pressure. I knew I had no interest in pursuing a relationship with her, but I figured it was early so what the heck. I gave my car to the valet and we headed in to the lobby bar. I asked Caroline to order drinks while I went to the restroom. When I came back out only a few minutes later Caroline was seated on one of the sofas in the lounge. She handed me my drink and raised her glass for a toast. "Salute!" and she then remarked, "Drink up!" She heartily downed her glass of wine.

I took a few more gulps of my martini and told her I really had to get going. When I stood up I realized something was wrong with me. I was dizzy and my eyesight was blurred. I struggled to keep my balance. Caroline saw my unsteadiness and told me I was in no condition to drive home. I remember hearing her say, "Come up to my room and sleep it off." I have no recollection of going up the elevator or seeing any other people around. It was like I was sleepwalking!

What I do remember though is waking up the next day. I found myself tied, spread-eagle to the bed. My wrists and ankles were handcuffed and tied to the bed posts. I was naked and had something stuffed in my mouth. Yet in a daze, my eyes searched the room. I was disoriented and confused, then I slowly became more aware of my situation.

"Good morning, sleepyhead," Caroline called as she entered the bedroom. "Did you have a good night's sleep?"

I mumbled.

"What's wrong? Cat got your tongue?"

I had a gag in my mouth and couldn't speak, but watched as she was gathering up her belongings. She then said she had already checked out and the maid should be coming around soon. She laughed and said I shouldn't hang around too long or the maid would see my little predicament. She laughed. She said she had to catch a plane and couldn't hang around any longer to chat and all the while that she was stuffing her belongings into a small suitcase. I watched in horror, but couldn't do anything. She thanked me for what turned out to be a very enjoyable evening even though it was a huge bore to begin with. She laughed. Then she told me I wouldn't remember any of the fun, but not to worry because she'd send me a video from her cell phone. "It really came out well," and she laughed again and set her suitcase and purse next to the door. She held up my business card, waiving it in one hand and saying she knew how to reach me and would send me the link to my first porn. "You were a real trooper last night. You took more than most men."

She came to the bedside and kissed my stuffed mouth, then unlocked one wrist cuff and laid a key on the nightstand and headed for the door. Her voice trailed behind her as she warned me not to tell anyone about the tryst because no one would ever believe I was an unwilling participant in the kinky lovemaking session. It would be a woman's word against the word of a big man. Furthermore, her identity for renting the room was completely fake. She was not from Washington. "Bye bye, sweetheart," and slammed the door closed. She was gone.

I'm not sure how long I laid motionless in that bed before I got my wits together and freed myself from the handcuffs and ripped the duct tape off my mouth. I realized I had been given a date rape drug. I felt sick. I was violated and humiliated, but at least I was alive. I dragged myself off the bed and found my clothes outside on the tiny balcony. My wallet was on the desk by the phone, money and credit cards missing. My expensive watch was missing. I felt beat up and exhausted the way you'd feel if you just went ten rounds in a boxing ring, but had no bruises or scratches anywhere on my body. I was just mentally defeated.

I couldn't decide whether to call the police, hotel security or just slip out of there unnoticed. I figured if I involved the authorities on any level I'd be even more humiliated by having to tell the story to strangers. There are more details too disgusting to tell that I wouldn't even anonymously reveal in this story, much less recount in a police interrogation. I was fearful that something like this could get into the newspaper. And further, I had no way of directing the authorities to Caroline since I had no phone number for her and our only correspondence had been via email. I decided to just get the hell out of that place.

It took several days afterwards before I felt recovered. I've never told this story to anyone before, but writing it out now helps give me some closure. I must stay anonymous to protect my reputation, but hope that by telling my story it will serve as a reminder to others how important it is to be cautious when dating new people. You just never know who you might run into on these online dating sites. If this could happen to a big guy like me, it could happen to anyone. I took myself off that dating site and never heard from Caroline again.

One of my favorite songs used to be Neil Diamond's "Sweet Caroline". I guarantee you I will never listen to that song again.

Take-Away: Assaults don't just happen to women. Men are also susceptible. If you have a bad feeling about someone, and something just doesn't feel right about that person, go with your gut. Don't worry about hurt feelings. More often than not, your instincts are right. And remember, don't ever leave your drink unguarded.

To Russia With Love

I met a great girl on *Match*. Her profile said she was from Miami and since I was living in Florida, she was only an hour's drive away. I could see from her site pictures, she was beautiful. She looked youthful for her age, late twenties, and had a unique quality about her that was different from other girls I had met from the Miami area who were typically sophisticated, model-types and spoiled with designer clothing, jewelry and cosmetic enhancements of every sort.

We developed an internet exchange and Natalya referred frequently to her Russian heritage. I found her sweet and innocent personality to be appealing, especially in the way she would greet me with her messaging each morning. As time went by, I told her that I wanted to see her and take her out for dinner. She thought that was funny. It wasn't until she told me that she was back in Russia that I understood her amusement over my invitation to meet.

As our little online romance began to blossom over weeks of time, I grew anxious to see her personally despite the distance between us. Her faithful morning messages kept my attention from wandering toward any other girls and I quit responding to other online prospects. Each of Natalya's messages came with a picture of her. They revealed so much of her beauty and playfulness. One autumn setting showed her rolling in a pile of golden-colored leaves. Another gorgeous shot had her playing in the snow wearing the cutest Russian hat. An especially eye-catching photo was of her doing cartwheels in a grassy meadow. I found myself daydreaming over those pictures and realized I was falling for her, but I had to remind myself those feelings might be all for naught because of the distance that separated us. Our emailing continued.

I learned that Natalya was a school teacher. She taught piano as well. She told me that she was very close to her parents and was an only child. I learned that she had a friend named Marina who was very skeptical of me, imagining me to be one of those American men who only wanted one thing from Natalya, a sexual partner. But the main thing I learned from Natalya was that she was really falling in love with me. She began signing off her letters with "Yours forever" or "Lovingly yours". Her writing expressed a belief that she had finally met her soul mate in me and that I was on her mind 24/7. She pledged that she had no interest in any other man.

It was about that time when she brought up the suggestion to come and see me. She told me she had some money saved and was going to a travel agent to find out what the process would be to come back to the States. The very next day she emailed. She expressed sadness and heartbroken despair because she didn't have enough money to pay for a ticket and the necessary papers. I asked her how much she needed and she itemized the costs for her train trip to the city, an overnight stay for processing paperwork and the roundtrip airfare to Miami, all total $2,000. I told her not to be sad because I would try to figure out some way to help finance the trip.

I told a friend of mine what was transpiring and she asked me if I had ever actually talked to Natalya on the phone. I confessed

I hadn't and was struck by her not-so-subtle lack of support for my Russian romance. She began filling my ear with what felt like painful daggers being plunged into my heart. She said she'd heard of scams that sounded just like this whole thing. "Your Natalya might not even be a real person," she fumed. "Your sweet little Natalya could be some guy pulling off a hoax just like that story in the news about the football player from Notre Dame, who ended up duped and publicly humiliated because he fell for a fictitious online romance." That got my attention.

Following my friend's eye-opening warning, I realized I should make an investigative effort to assure myself of the truth. I emailed Natalya and told her that I had very good news. I buttered up a little story that I was off for the summer and, since I had always wanted to visit Russia, she should give me her address and I would meet with my travel agent to plan my trip to Russia for the summer.

I never heard from Natalya again.

Take-Away: There are plenty of scammers online. Do not send money, tickets, or anything of monetary value unless you confirm that the person you've been corresponding to is who they say they are. Talk to the person on the phone…..skype. Do not rely on texting or email to verify. Meeting in person is always better if possible.

"The Bad"

I've Been Hacked

My first online date was in the City on a Friday night. Since I had just signed up for my dating service on the prior Wednesday and immediately began receiving some fifty messages a day from eligible girls, you can well imagine how my masculine energies became immediately supercharged. All the feminine attention was making me feel like a world class stallion! I was off to the races in my social life again, but as you will see from my story, I got way caught up in the excitement and ignored an online dating rule by putting the cart before the old horse. I jumped into my first date with blinders on.

Taking the train in that night, I met my date at the designated restaurant. She looked just like her picture from the website, and we enjoyed a nice dinner while hashing through all the usual "getting to know you" conversation. She then invited me back to her place for an after dinner drink. Although I was tempted to accept her invitation, I declined and explained that I had to catch the last train back to Connecticut, because I had an early morning business appointment. She insisted that I stay, so I figured I had 30 minutes maximum that I could stay.

So, there I was in her apartment. She poured me a drink and then excused herself, leaving me alone in the den. She returned to the dimly lit room after ten or fifteen minutes wearing lingerie, the kind that is transparent from top to bottom, and started coming on to me. Oh, I was tempted alright, what with that lingerie in my face, but something about this gal was making me uncomfortable. I backed off and used the last train home as my lame excuse to end the evening. Polite as I knew how, I told her I'd have to take a rain check, then set my glass down and headed toward the door. When she took hold of my arm to stop me, I began to think she was definitely a little crazy and that I would pay dearly if I went for the instant gratification she was offering. I said I really did have to go.

She suddenly became furious as I opened the door to leave. She cursed and threw a pillow at me, hitting me in the back. Then, of all things, began hurling Hershey kisses from a candy bowl at me, peppering the back of my trench coat like bullets from a machine gun as I walked down the hall. Last noise I heard as the elevator door closed behind me was a loud door slam and breaking glass from inside her apartment. I got out just in time and as I was going down the elevator, felt thankful for the willpower to leave when I did. I caught the last train home.

Next day I went online to see how many new messages had come in, but oddly there were none. "How can that be?" I wondered. "Go from fifty a day to zero just because it's Saturday?" Sunday and Monday brought the same result and then late Tuesday I had "1 New Message." With great zeal, I opened it up. It was from a girl who asked if I had read my profile lately. She suggested I check it.

I had a bad feeling as I went directly to my personal profile in the site. My photo was there, my stats were correct, but under the description tab was something new. At the question, "What do you like doing on a first date?" was a new answer that I had not typed in. It said, "I enjoy taking girls back to my home, tying them up naked in my dungeon and raping them."

No wonder I wasn't getting any messages now! I felt so embarrassed, even after quickly deleting the answer. I realized someone had hacked into my profile and changed the answer to make me look like a predator, and after some thought had little doubt who the culprit was, the girl from my first online date. She must have guessed my password , my dog's name that I talked about at length during our dinner that night.

I reported her to the dating service, demanded that my profile be removed immediately from the site, and I never went back into that website again. It was a bad experience for sure.

Take-Away: Don't be so eager to jump in bed with the first person you meet....even though the opportunity may present itself. And don't use your pet's name for a password. It's too obvious.

What's Your Husband Doing Here?

It is a moonlit Saturday night and I am cruising south to Miami for a dinner date. While thinking about the young lady I connected with on my singles site only five days earlier, I hope the sixty mile drive to meet her for dinner will be worth the effort. Before I know it, I have arrived. I hand my BMW keys to the parking valet then pause to straighten my tie and relax myself as I walk toward the front doors of the posh restaurant. Soft lighting filtered through the glass façade of the place creating a romantic aura and mirroring my dapper reflection. I think I look pretty good so I pull my self-confidence together and saunter in to meet the young lady face to face.

Our greeting in the lobby is pleasant, and we are promptly seated at a nice table on the outside patio next to the railing beside the water's edge. Our drinks and appetizers are served. She has on a pretty dress that is very low cut and appealing, and although we have a lot in common to talk about, my second Grey Goose quickly begins kicking in and that low cut dress starts quietly whispering in my ear, making it difficult for me to concentrate on the conversation.

So, our meals are served and half way through my veal parmesan, a pleasant sounding gentleman shows up at our table and asks, "Are you enjoying your dinner?"

Not wanting to be interrupted from my luscious food and female, I flash a glance and answer, "Everything's great." My curt response is intended to dismiss his intrusion but it doesn't, and he continues to hover over the table, stepping even closer toward my chair.

In a seriously deep voice he now says, "That's nice. So, you're enjoying spending your evening with my wife?"

That got my attention. I look up at the large man who is now staring me down. "Your wife?" I retort with an insulted tone. He begins flexing his chest muscles. With that, my date says, "Frank, what are you doing here?"

Then, lowering his dark, bushy eyebrows and rapidly shifting his squinted eyes back and forth between the two of us, he says, "I should be asking you two the same thing!"

My mind begins to race and I feel a surge of pressure welling up in my neck. I thought about the waterway on the other side of the railing next to me and shudder to imagine it might be my only escape route. Equally horrifying is the thought he might be intending to throw me over. The big guy towers above me and I shift back in my chair in an attempt to put a little more space between us. As his posturing becomes even more animated, I have a sickening feeling that the situation is going to end badly. Frank asks, "how did you guys meet?"

My instincts tell me not to tell the truth, since internet dating would sound incriminating, so I blurt out an impromptu story. Shrouding myself with the look of an innocent man, I answer, "I was having drinks at the bar and asked your wife, I mean Natalie, to join me. I had no idea she was married. She had no wedding ring on and was sitting by herself. Hey, I'm not the enemy here, buddy."

With that, Frank looks at his wife to confirm what I hope will be my lifesaving alibi, but she has buried her face in her hands and says nothing. I can tell Frank is debating whether he should punch me on the spot or back off, believing I'm not guilty of participating in infidelities. There is a moment of silence. Then to my good fortune, the Florence Nightingale of waitresses appears at our table. She asks if we are enjoying our meal and if there is anything she can get for us. The voice in my head screams, "Yes! Yes! Call the police," but I hold my tongue and cling to a small bit of composure, quickly deciding on the more dignified response, "Check, please."

I promptly get up and follow my rescuing angel to the waitress station where I pay the tab to expedite my exit. Guarding not to look back, I summon the valet for my car and speed away as fast as possible. The long drive home gives me plenty of time to think about what has just happened and what could have happened, but I am breathing easier now that the romantic breezes of Miami are behind me and blowing me safely out of town in the direction of Palm Beach.

My phone rings just as I get home and it is Natalie, my married date. She apologizes for her husband showing up at dinner and explains how Frank is fighting against their divorce. She says he has been stalking her and it is not the first time he has run off one of her dinner dates. I ask her why she didn't warn me ahead of time, and she confesses she had become so attracted to me through our internet connection that she was afraid we would never get together if she told. Her fears were valid because had I known, I probably would not have agreed to the date. She apologizes for her nondisclosure and thanks me for the nice time, despite it ending up with the uninvited third party. She then suggests that we could safely get together another time if I wanted, and without hesitation I bark, "Are you kidding me?"

Natalie and I dated for about two months.

Take-Away: Don't date married people. There are plenty of unattached out there. You're just looking for trouble, and usually, nothing good will ever come out of it…just the opposite.

Husband Has Anger Issues

A friend of mine referred me to a website that specialized in married women who were looking for an affair. Can you believe there's actually a site like that? There is, and by next year at this time there will probably be sites for everybody who is looking for anything you can imagine! At any rate, I had just ended a long term relationship and wasn't looking to jump into any new commitment, so I figured finding a "friend with benefits" would be the emotionally safe option for companionship and, well, you know, those carnal requirements. I found a lady on the site that appealed to me.

Her name was Suzanne and we had our first date at a downtown café about thirty miles from my home. It turned out that not only did she and I live in the same town, but I had actually met her years ago with her husband whom I had done business with. I always thought she was a beautiful woman.

She explained that she and her husband were legally separated, and for that reason had gone on the site. We had an instant attraction and began our affair. It wasn't an affair for me because I wasn't seeing anyone and technically not for her either because she was separated, but she didn't see it that way. In her eyes, she was having an affair since she was still legally married. I insisted she wasn't doing anything wrong, but she explained that her husband was definitely the jealous type and, even though he no longer lived at the house they shared, he would kill anyone (not literally) if he thought they were screwing his wife.

With all that said, we decided it would be best if we met a couple times a week in hotels miles away from our home town. We planned to always drive separately and that I would book the room before calling to let her know the room number once I was settled in. Since I'd never had a relationship like this before, I discovered it was kind of exciting and dangerous. I liked the secrecy.

After seeing each other for months, I talked Suzanne into meeting me at my house. I instructed her to park her car in my garage, and since I had a long circular driveway, it seemed like a safe haven. And it was, until one evening.

My home, which is tucked away on the end of a quiet cul-de-sac, boasts a huge picture window on the landing of a grand staircase. It can be seen clearly from the street, but privacy is not an issue because there are only three other homes on the block with very few cars that come or go. One weekend when Suzanne was staying over, I was coming down the staircase in the middle of the night. The chandelier was dimly lit so I didn't think twice about anyone seeing me in my boxers. But on that night, just as I was half way down, imagine my shock when all the sudden the huge window completely shattered as if impacted from the outside. It literally exploded. I covered my face with my hands and ducked.

I called the police. Initially, I imagined a bat had hit the window. However, it didn't take long for the authorities who arrived at the scene to discover that a bullet from a high powered rifle had come through the glass causing it to shatter. Their investigation then turned into an attempted murder case. The suspect turned out to be Suzanne's husband.

I don't want to go into what actually happened to Suzanne's husband, but I will say his jealousy got the better of him. I think he learned a valuable lesson that brought with it some serious consequences.

Take-Away: Cheating or fooling around with a married woman can be dangerous business. You'd better weigh it all out carefully and decide if it's worth the risk. As for me, I've decided to stay on more conventional dating sites. I don't want to ever be accused of breaking up a home and family.

Grossly Misrepresented

A young lady goes to a restaurant to meet her internet date for the first time. She is pretty excited because the guy's photographs in the website showed him to be handsome and fairly athletic. He explained that she would be able to recognize him at the designated eatery because he would be wearing a navy blue sport jacket.

When she arrived, she paused in the lobby and looked across the dining room before finally spotting a gentleman in a navy blue jacket with his back in her direction seated at a table. Since it was the only navy blue jacket in the place, she approached to introduce herself. As he turned in his seat to greet her, she saw that the man's face was covered with scabs. His unsightly appearance was so egregious that she flinched from the unexpected shock of it, and then quickly cast her eyes around the room to hide her reaction. She was in disbelief, hardly believing this could be the same guy from the profile in the website. It was however.

He motioned her to sit down at his table and they began some small talk. The young lady quickly decided the only polite thing for her to do was try to make the best of the unsettling surprise. She took a deep breath and promptly ordered a stiff drink. He was already sipping on a cocktail, and from the looks of its greenish color, she had no clue what it was. She didn't ask. Taking another deep breath, she dug deep to muster a pleasant smile for him as they chatted face-to-face across their small table. She intended to make it through dinner quickly so she could get the heck out of there as soon as possible, hoping not to hurt his feelings.

Half way through their meal, her date excused himself to go to the bathroom. She watched as he struggled to stand up from his chair. She tried to hide her double-take of him as he waddled away in the fashion of a hog-tied penguin. His legs were so bulbously fat he could barely negotiate the aisle between the tables and chairs in the room. And just when she thought all that was too strenuous for her to bare, she noticed a large tumor behind his left ear that looked like a cauliflower growth. He disappeared into the restroom hallway and was finally out of her sight.

Now sitting alone, she blinked hard the way a person does when they simply cannot believe what they are seeing. A mental vision flashed into her mind from the movie about the elephant man. She surmised this guy must have come down with the same malady since his earlier years when those handsome pictures in the website had been taken. Her nervous system was by now a wreck and she fought the urge to get up and run away while he was gone. She didn't.

He returned to the table and somehow she managed to keep herself emotionally glued together until the meal was finished. What helped her through the time was that she mostly stared down at her plate while obsessively cutting every piece of food into tiny, tiny bites which she rapidly devoured. It was tedious and tiring work for her to do this, but the only polite way to avoid looking at his face.

At the end, he said he would call her so they could get together again soon. She shook his hand and left.

Several days later he texted her saying he would love to see her again. She responded by saying she was going to be out of town on vacation for several weeks with girlfriends. She assumed that would be the end of it between them…

…but a searing reply came back. "You're a liar. I don't believe you're going anywhere, much less with your girlfriends. You're nothing but another stupid #%@ and fricking whore. Why don't you go die somewhere because no one will ever miss you. Go f…k yourself!"

The girl was quivering in her boots after reading his text. She knew she couldn't have been nicer to him, even in spite of the fact that he had misrepresented himself. She went into a slow burn over the insulting text for days afterward. *I should have walked out on the jerk the second he left the table to go to the restroom!*

Take-Away: There are too many creeps out there. Many are gross liars and some are GROSS people! If you're uncomfortable with a certain someone or situation, tell them you have an emergency at home and excuse yourself. Better be safe than sorry.

Butter Face

Talk about deception! I've been on *Match.com* for a couple of years now, and I realize that everyone is trying to appear at their best to get attention. So what if they lie a little bit on their profiles to enhance their chances for love? I confess that I have two white lies on mine. One is that I make over $250,000 annual income, although I hope to someday, and the other one which is no biggie is that I say I'm 40 instead of 50. Oh, and there's one more detail that I stretched the truth on. I say that I'm divorced even though I've never been legally married, but I really don't consider that a lie because I've had several long term relationships that were almost like being married. I just don't want to give the impression that I am commitment phobic.

But my little lies don't even come close to equaling a deception like this, a woman who showed pictures of herself in a bikini, evening gown and workout clothes representing herself to have a body to die for. Diane did just that and I fell for it. In each of her photos the face was distorted and made blurry. When I spoke with Diane, she explained she didn't want people at her work, her boss or friends to know she was online looking for men. I get that. So, since she seemed really nice on the phone I arranged a dinner date with her on a Friday night. She told me she was really looking forward to meeting me in person.

She said she wanted to make a good first impression and was having a hard time deciding on the right dress to wear, then began to describe the one she was considering. She asked my opinion. She said it was a little black dress with a sheer, see-through opening to her lower back and v-line cut front. I imagined something like that would highlight that gorgeous body of hers and be appropriate for the restaurant. I told her it sounded perfect, and that I couldn't wait to see it, I mean her.

I made dinner reservations at the Capitol Grill for 8 p.m. and Diane told me she'd meet me in the bar. She had arrived before me and it was easy to pick her out from the crowd because she was the only single woman sitting at the bar wearing a black dress. As I approached, her back was toward me and I felt certain I had the right girl.

"Hello, Diane."

When she turned around I was blown away, and I mean blown away as in a bad, bad explosion! This woman had a knock out body but a face that looked like a spooky pumpkin at Halloween. She looked like Susan Boyle, the opera singer who became a sensation for her amazing voice on the television program *America's Got Talent*, but who was unfortunately very homely. I did everything I could not to show my shock and disappointment over Diane's facial appearance. It was a horribly uncomfortable moment. Her Playboy Bunny's body was to die for, but aside from that she was really a woof!

After greeting her, I did everything I could to make our evening enjoyable. We had a nice dinner and Diane really couldn't have been a nicer person. It turned out that a client of mine was eating dinner at a table right next to us and as he was leaving he came by and introduced his wife to me. I introduced Diane to both of them. We exchanged pleasantries. I'm certain next time I see this man he's going to say something like, "Nice dinner date you had, but WHAT WERE YOU THINKING?"

I never saw Diane again and actually feel a little bad about that. She was so sweet and kind. She was well-dressed and poised in every sense. She had a sexy body, but her face (Butter Face) wasn't happening in my world.

Yoga Bear

While reviewing the women's profiles on the website, I came across a lady who was a yoga instructor. She had great pics of herself, giving the impression that she was a pretty hot chick. So I made a date with her and showed up at Mizner Park in Boca Raton for our dinner. Greeting her with a handshake, I was horrified that she looked nothing like her pictures, and to make matters worse, she was at least fifty pounds heavier than the sexy images she had posted. Most certainly the photos were at least ten years old.

Interestingly, she had brought her dog along for the date. He was a lab named "Bear". Now he was a cute, cute chocolate lab and since I am a dog-lover, I found it easy to lavish my pent-up affections and attention on him. I smartly requested an outside table so the dog could stay with us, and Bear made himself at home next to my feet throughout the evening. I even ordered a full chicken breast dinner for him. My date, Jennette, thought this was an especially sweet gesture on my part. Little did she know I was secretly consoling my disappointed-self with the idea that buying dinner for Bear was clearly more appealing than dinner with her.

Our conversation was minimal and after saying goodbye, I knew for certain I would not be asking her out for a second date, mainly because she had misrepresented herself in the website and also

I had no attraction to her. I have, however, considered calling her again to ask if she'd allow me to take Bear for a Sunday afternoon in the park. I'm just not sure how Miss Yoga Instructor might take it when I say I only want to see Bear again.

Take-Away: Beware of profiles mentioning how often the person works out. This applies to both men and women. Often times, this fact is very deceiving as you will or have discovered already. You would think that a woman with Yoga in her name would be in pretty good shape. Not always. This is a HUGE misrepresentation which is rampant on even the most popular sites.

Call Me Maybe?

I've been online dating off and on for several years now and have met a lot of nice girls. But during that time I have also encountered loads of misrepresentation. Outdated photos, incorrect age, body weight discrepancies and untrue marital status seem to be what I've bumped into more than on occasion. I eventually made it my practice to completely ignore new messages that didn't come with a profile photo or at least the lady's willingness to send me a picture of herself separately…until now.

Marcy was the exception. She lived in New York City, Gramercy Park to be exact. She explained in the beginning that she hadn't posted a picture because she had a high profile job and didn't want people at her work to know she was online. I could understand that and had actually heard the same explanation once before from a professional lady, so Marcy's reason didn't set off any red flags for me. What did worry me slightly was the fact that when I asked her if she would email me her photo, she told me she'd rather not, but assured me there was nothing to worry about. She gave me her measurements, told me that she was a brunette and that most men find her to be very attractive. She said, "Not to worry, Dave. You'll find me attractive. I guarantee it!"

She seemed so self-confident with her beauty that I figured what the heck and admonished myself for being so shallow. I agreed to my first online blind date.

Marcy gave me her apartment building address as well as her apartment number. That was unusual in that ordinarily on a first date, I would meet the lady in the lobby of her building. I had never had a first date invite me directly to her unit, but self-confident Marcy did!

When I got to the building I was told by the doorman that she was expecting me. He showed me to the elevators. Up to the sixth floor and I found myself anxiously standing at her door. I was nervous. I had no idea what she looked like and was praying she was going to be a beauty. I knocked and the door opened slowly, very slowly. I felt suspended in a time warp before I finally saw her face and when our eyes met, I was hardly impressed. I was shockingly disappointed! How in the world did she have so much confidence in her appearance when she looked like a plain Jane school teacher? She reminded me of Adrienne in the movie "Rocky". I'm not saying Adrienne when she got her makeover, but the Adrienne who Rocky just met, mousey -looking with glasses, and mousey-looking is not my idea of attractive. Call me shallow, I don't care. I was disappointed in her appearance.

After greeting each other, we took a walk through Gramercy Park to our destination, a small café. I tried to make the most of our date without showing my disappointment, and she was without question a very nice girl, just not my type. I walked her home and into the lobby of her building where she asked if I wanted to come upstairs. I thanked her for the invitation but said I had to get back home to let my dog out. She gave me a look of doubt. She must have thought I didn't even have a dog, but of course I did and whether she believed it or not doesn't matter. Then I went on to say what a nice time I had and how great it was to meet her. I gave her a little hug and said, "I'll call you… maybe." I couldn't believe that "maybe" actually came out of my mouth. It was suppose to be just a subconscious thought.

"Maybe? What kind of bullshit is that"? She says out loud.

I was taken by surprise with that coming out of her mouth. I had no idea a plain Jane school teacher was allowed to talk that way, did you? There were several people in the lobby who turned and looked our direction, embarrassing me beyond belief. And I wasn't sure if she said bullshit because she didn't think I had a dog or if she didn't think I would call her again so I came back at her with, "What do you mean bullshit?"

She said she knew I wasn't her type and that I had no intention of calling her again, much less asking her out on a second date. What could I say? She was right. I wasn't planning on speaking to her again; I just thought it was nicer to say what I said than something like, "Hey, have a nice life, witch."

I shrugged my shoulders and smiled, "Maybe I'll surprise you."

With that she turned to the elevators and sarcastically replied, "Whatever." I never did call Marcy again.

Take-Away: Don't ever invite your date to your home or apartment on the first date. You're only looking for trouble. Don't say anything that you don't really mean. If you don't plan to see your date ever again, just say it was nice meeting them. Don't ever say you'll call when you have no intention of doing so... even if "maybe" you might call them.

That's My Baby

I've always had good luck using the dating site called *What's Your Price*. It's a site that profiles gorgeous young women who will accompany you to dinner, a fundraiser or any other legitimate purpose. To a man, these ladies would be considered arm candy. A guy can walk into a room with one of these dates and feel proud of the lady on his arm because of her class and looks. All you have to do is negotiate your price prior to the date and you get a beautiful companion.

One weekend I was in town and negotiated the price for a date with a young lady from the site. Her pictures were beautiful. There were some bikini shots, some nightclub shots and one shot of her in a baby doll lingerie outfit. What a sexy girl, I thought. I agreed to pay her a price of $150 to accompany me to dinner, and we then arranged to meet at a waterfront restaurant in Pompano, Florida.

My date, Elise, was to join me at 8:30 on a Saturday evening. I arrived early. Although we had never spoken on the phone, we had been messaging back and forth for several days prior. I waited on the patio feeling a bit anxious to meet her in person. I sipped a nice dry martini and watched the boats on the intracoastal pass by. I was finally relaxing just about the time I got a text from her. She said she was running fifteen minutes late. No problem.

Twenty minutes went by and I noticed a crowd of people coming in the front doors of the restaurant. It was a big rowdy group celebrating someone's birthday and at the tail end of the group was a face I recognized, Elise. No question about the face, but what I didn't recognize was any other part of her. She was pregnant… and I don't mean just a little bit pregnant either. She was dressed in a white dress, maternity-style, and actually looked amazingly stylish with a scarf draped around her shoulders and hair pulled up. Her jewelry, nice tan and shoes really looked attractive…but she really looked pregnant too!

So, here I am waiting for my $150 beautiful dinner date and what did I get, two for the price of one? Am I supposed to call that a deal?

I watched her as she paused in the lobby. She was looking around, obviously waiting for me to spot her first. Had I thought it possible, I would have sneaked right by her and out the front door, never to be seen again, but there was no escape route so I walked over to introduce myself to the misrepresented mother-to-be. I guess Elise figured nondisclosure of her condition was OK. But from my viewpoint, she not only misrepresented herself, she failed to disclose a materially relevant fact! Hey, I'm a Realtor. You can't do that in real estate. You have to make FULL disclosure.

At any rate, Elise says hello to me and doesn't say a word about her condition. I don't either. We took our table next to the water, and I genuinely considered jumping in and swimming all the way to Cuba, but I didn't. The only gentlemanly option at this point was to stay put and make the most of the situation. I paid Elise her $150 and decided to ignore the white elephant in the room.

But by the end of our dinner, I will admit I thoroughly enjoyed her company and conversation. She turned out to be a real delight, and she did finally reveal to me the story of her pregnancy. She said the baby's father wouldn't be around for the birth because he didn't want her to have the baby. He was a guy she had dated for six months and had no intention of supporting her. Their relationship was over.

I have little doubt she'd have made the date with me or any other guy unless she really needed the income. So, even though I felt a little taken advantage of, I was glad she hadn't given me full disclosure up front. Had she, I'm certain I would never have made the date with her. But as it turned out, I liked her a lot and told her I wanted the best for her. I told her I'd like to see her again after the baby was born.

I recently found out she had a little girl, and I can't wait to see both of them sometime soon.

Brother Can You Spare A Dime?

I made a date with this girl I met on the internet and we met at Seasons 52. The place is a casually sophisticated grill and wine bar known for its healthy and low calorie indulgences. It seemed she was completely comfortable meeting for our first date at a place like this that offered an award-winning international wine list and pricey culinary excellence.

We were both relaxed and enjoying a glass of imported Gewürztraminer while sharing the most excellent stuffed artichoke leaves when she popped the inevitable question, "so, what are you looking for in a relationship?"

"Well," I began, "a nice, classy girl to spend some time with, someone who is funny, low key and likes to travel. That's about it."

She smiled and said that sounded good. I then returned the question to her. "I'm basically looking for the same," she said, "but with one added thing." After a long pause, I gestured as if to say, "OK, and what would that be?"

There was another long pause before she said, "well, I just got laid off from my work."

Now feeling pulled to the edge of my seat and a little annoyed at her stringing out the point I said, "so what's the added thing? You need a job?"

She shook her head and said she had a bunch of resumes out. She thought she would be able to find a job fairly quickly but, "In the meantime…" There was then a long, silent pause as she pulled out a handful of bills from her purse, fanning them out on the table in front of me. There were credit card bills, Florida Power and Lighting bills, her BMW payment coupon booklet, cable, cell service and a red delinquent stamp on a paper that said "Notice To Vacate." She proceeded to explain that she just needed a little help with her bills until she was able to get on her feet again. I was speechless. Then she gently placed her hand on my thigh.

I'm not a hundred percent sure, but I think the expression on her face was saying, "You take care of my needs and I'll take care of yours."

Never saw that one coming!

I'm Mad As Hell And I'm Not Going To Take It Anymore

I did something the other day that I'm not proud of, but it's something that I needed to finally do. I met a girl on *Match*.com whose name was Lydia. Lydia seemed like someone I could really relate to. She was in the real estate business, so was I. She loved dogs, so did I. She was a world traveler, so am I. So we decided to meet right away at a restaurant called *Abe and Louies*. Lydia had one picture of herself online and it was a bit blurry and distorted, but from what I could see, she looked attractive. When I was talking to her on the phone, she complained that it was the only recent picture she had without another person in it. She claimed she didn't know how to use Photoshop, but assured me that she was a strikingly beautiful brunette.

I've been deceived before by girls who looked nothing like their online photo, and I have often bought dinners for these women just because I didn't have the heart to tell them that they drastically misrepresented themselves. Those dinners cost me at least a hundred dollars each time and I remember many times leaving the restaurant at the end of the date feeling that I had been ripped off. And I'm not talking about the restaurant; I'm talking about the deceptive women! Some of them were obviously much older than they said, some were much heavier and some even deliberately hid behind the veil of their website. Then there were some who had obviously unattractive features that they must have known would eliminate them from getting invited on a dinner date.

But Lydia appeared to be attractive from the looks of her one photo and seemed sweet on the phone so I was looking forward to meeting her in person. However, just as a precaution I decided to take an extreme measure to protect myself from being duped again. Under the theory of "fool me once shame on you, fool me twice shame on me", I came up with a secret plan. I told Lydia that I would be wearing a dark blue suit and red tie when we met at the restaurant. She said she would be wearing a red dress and boots. We were to meet at 5:30 that afternoon in the bar. It was a date.

Just as I was pulling into the parking lot at the restaurant, Lydia texted me to say she had found a seat at the end of the bar. I told her I was running a little late. That was my stall for some time so I could secretly check her out before introducing myself. When I walked in, the place was crowded but I saw her right away. She stuck out like a sore thumb in that red dress and her large body spilling over the edges of the bar stool. She had to have been at least fifty pounds heavier than she claimed to be.

Yes, I'd been deceived again. I determined I wasn't going to waste my time or money on someone that I had absolutely no interest in getting to know better. Call me shallow. Call me heartless if you wish, but I intended to do the unthinkable at that point. I quietly turned around and left unnoticed.

People, have a heart for me here. I realize that looks don't tell a woman's whole picture, but she lied to me and everyone else on that website by posting a false picture of what she looks like now. I'm fed up with being taken advantage of. I'm simply saying, "Nope. No more. Nada!"

As I was driving away, I texted Lydia and told her I was so sorry that I had been detained with a client at the office and wouldn't be able to make our date for dinner. She said she understood. I told her I'd call to reschedule, but of course that was a lie. Do you think I should have told her the truth? I didn't want to risk any confrontation because I don't handle that sort of thing well. I do think she should be told the truth, but I don't want to be the one to hurt her feelings. I never spoke to Lydia again.

Once A Cheater

I met Jason a year ago online. When we first started dating, he was great fun to be with. All our friends thought we made a good couple. The one thing we both loved to do was travel and Jason was generous in paying for some really terrific trips. Our last one was to Cabo San Lucas, Mexico. The ocean and scenery there are beautiful. Jason especially loved the late night beer bars we hung out at, festive and casual in Mexican style. I particularly enjoyed the food we had while there, fresh ocean catch every day.

From early on in our relationship, Jason gave me his American Express card to use and I never abused it. The most I ever charged on it was for a cocktail dress, a pair of shoes and some lingerie, nothing extravagant by most standards. We had a trusting relationship living together at his place, but I kept my apartment downtown as security just in case. Good thing I did.

I started getting a little suspicious of Jason after our trip to Cabo when he began working late more often. We weren't having as much sex as we used to, which was not by my choice. I had always heard women intuitively know when their man is cheating and my instincts were beginning to tell me something was going on with him behind the scenes, despite no clear cut evidence. Other than working late and less sex, he seemed to be normal. "Maybe," I reasoned to myself, "I was letting my imagination get the best of me." Classic denial, right?

Then one Saturday afternoon I was going to the dry cleaners and grabbed some of Jason's shirts. It wasn't until I noticed lipstick smudges on one collar and a shirt sleeve that my earlier suspicions were confirmed. It was the most horrible moment of my life seeing the evidence of my cheating boyfriend. It was a painful reality check that smacked me square in the face. I suppose it would have been worse on me had I not already had a glimpse of some yellow flags, but the emotional devastation was still overwhelming.

I called my girlfriend, wailing and sobbing about my discovery, "What should I do? Should I confront him?"

"No way!" she commanded. "I'll be right there to get you. We'll get even."

Over coffee she advised me not to mention a word of it to him. She insisted that from the time boys are young they are programmed to never never never confess to infidelity. Confronting Jason with my evidence would serve no useful purpose. I believed what she said and after I was finished with a few more tears, she took me shopping and made me buy myself the most beautiful and expensive handbag I'd ever seen. It was a Hermes Birkin bag. I paid for it with Jason's American Express card.

I broke up with him two weeks later, never really giving a reason either. I wanted to make sure I got out before his credit card bill came in, and when it did he called me up screaming like an idiot. That's when I blasted him about being a cheater. He threatened to have me arrested for using his card, but my girlfriend said I had nothing to worry about. It's been months now and I've not heard from Jason since.

Till Death Do Us Part

I met a great guy on the *Seeking Arrangement* site. He is CEO of a large firm in New York City and commutes from his home in Chicago. From the first time we spoke on the phone, I found him to be both charming and funny. His name is Edward.

By way of background, Edward told me the sad story of his wife's death from cancer some six months earlier. He admitted that he had been lonely since her passing, but felt it was much too soon to entertain any sort of serious relationship. He wanted to be completely up front with his intentions and explained that he was only looking for companionship with no promise of any future commitment. He wanted to be with a woman who was young, beautiful and most importantly had no children and available to get away on a moment's notice for dates and trips. I liked what I heard and I fit the bill.

We had our first date in New York City, which is where I lived. After just three dates, it was clear to both of us that we were an excellent companion matchup. Edward then invited me to live in his corporate apartment in the City and I accepted. The only stipulation he placed on my living there was that I could not be seeing any other men and would devote my time exclusively to him whenever he was in town. I had no problem agreeing to the arrangement. We had already settled the matter of my weekly allowance, so I was purring like a kitten the day I left my tiny efficiency and set up housekeeping in his luxurious upscale apartment.

In the beginning, Edward came into the City about twice a month. For both of us, it was like a honeymoon each time he arrived. He took me to great restaurants, Broadway plays, gallery openings and on one occasion to a special business event where he was the keynote speaker. That event set the stage for moving our relationship to a different level.

His dinner speaking engagement was held in a large ballroom at the Waldorf. It was a fancy black tie occasion and Edward wanted me to really look classy and beautiful to impress his colleagues. He gave me his credit card to go shopping for what he called a Julia Roberts' showoff gown. Yes, I'd seen the movie and knew exactly how he wanted me to dress. I took the card and went shopping, buying an expensive red dress and shoes. I also bought some glitzy jewelry that wasn't terribly expensive, but secretly hoped he might surprise me with something more, like diamonds, the way Richard Gere did in the movie. I even had my hair done like Julie Roberts just for the fun of it and Edward behaved giddy as heck over me when I walked out of the bedroom that night dressed for the event. Unfortunately, he didn't surprise me with any diamond jewelry.

On the way to his speaking engagement, Edward explained that there would be over five hundred people in attendance and I would not be seated with him. He also said that due to the large crowd expected to be there, I should wait for him in a taxi out front if we didn't find each other when the event adjourned.

Once we arrived at the venue, he was escorted away and I was left to find my way to a table at the back of room that was designated for guests. I took a seat and spent the entire evening with ten other young people. I felt like I was at the kids' table and bored beyond belief. On one break during the evening, Edward made his way to where I was sitting and asked if I was enjoying myself. My sour attitude was obvious and he promised he'd make it up to me. That made me feel a little better, but when I couldn't find him after the event and ended up circling the block in a taxi for forty-five minutes, I began to wonder if he was ashamed to be seen with me. I was pretty sullen that night and he left for Chicago early the next morning.

The following week I received an airline ticket to St. Barts from Edward. That really lifted my spirits and I could hardly wait to meet him there for a three day vacation together. It turned out to be an amazing trip. On the last night of our romantic get-away, he gave me a beautiful pair of diamond earrings. I couldn't have been happier. I realized I was falling for him and began to think he was the perfect guy for me.

Then it happened.

Edward left St. Barts the next morning. He had only been gone for about an hour when the hotel phone rang in our suite. It was a woman's voice and she asked for Edward. At first I thought it was housecleaning. Then she asked, "Who is this?" I felt intimidated by the commanding tone in her voice and responded with the same question back to her, "Who is this?"

"Beverly, Edward's wife."

My brain went into overload and I was confused for a few dizzy moments. I had the urge to say, "I thought you were dead," but realized how crazy that was, so I did the only thing a girl could do in my situation. I hung up.

Needless to say, the lingering aroma of my wonderful vacation in St. Barts with my generous and romantic Edward quickly became overwhelmed by a bitter stench. I knew I couldn't get him on the phone because he was already in the air back to Chicago, so I left him a very nasty voicemail telling him that it appeared his wife had had a full recovery from her death and was looking for him. I spent the rest of the day crying and couldn't wait to catch my flight out and leave the island.

Edward and I spoke the following day. He apologized for lying to me and explained that Beverly had thrown him out of their home and he was living in an apartment in Chicago, now legally separated. He told me he would put a ring on my finger the moment their divorce was final and wanted me to stay in the New York apartment.

Maybe I'm naïve, but I love him and have decided to stay. Two months have passed since that event, and he comes to the City much more frequently now. Although I still don't have a ring on my finger, I believe it's going to come. I'll keep you posted.

AOL: Always On Line

I've had two long term relationships with guys who I have met online. Both relationships ended for the same reason. It seemed that no matter how happy and satisfied my men were with me, they seemed to believe there was someone better out there that they wanted to experiment with or get to know. Let me explain.

About a year ago I had been dating a guy named Ted for weeks. We were inseparable. We did everything together from grocery shopping to laundry. It wasn't because I necessarily wanted to but we just naturally fell into this totally comfortable flow with each other. One day while Ted had stepped out to go on an appointment I went into his office to look for a picture we had taken together. I thought I'd get it framed. I noticed that he had left his computer screen on and when I looked closer realized he had also left a website open. It happened to be the same dating site he and I originally met on.

Obviously curiosity got the best of me and I began exploring further. I found that he had not only been getting messages from women all over the world but was answering all of them. I knew I should have packed it up and left immediately, but I didn't. I read on. He was making dates with women. The messages showed confirmed dates, times and places and the most recent one was for that very afternoon at a restaurant close to us. He lied to me. He wasn't at an appointment at all; he was on a date with some babe named Bianca. I was furious now and like any crazed woman began grabbing all of my belongings, then threw them in my car and left. No note. No explanation. I just didn't want to see the cheating bum again. I don't even want to know if he was physically unfaithful to me either! I was out of there.

My next relationship ended just a month ago. Once again, I thought I had met the guy of my dreams. We spent most of our time on his boat and I had an amazing summer with him. Once again, I thought everything between he and I was great and once again, I thought we were an inseparable and happy couple.

After about two months of dating I noticed that Jack was on his computer a lot. Since I had a lingering trust issue, I had never allowed myself to assume all Jack said was the truth, the whole truth and nothing but the truth. Despite the fact that he consistently complimented me and told me I was the most sexually pleasing girl he had ever dated, I was still secretly guarded. But now that it seemed he was on the computer more often, I decided to test his loyalty without him knowing. I decided to go onto my phone and pull up the dating website where Jack and I first met to see if he was still active. I wanted to know too the last time he was on it. Well, bust my britches, knock my socks off and shoot me in the head! He had been on the site just the previous day.

It was all so perplexing because we had spent the entire day together. I didn't understand how this fit. So I decided I wasn't going bottle up my feelings and stuff it this time. I confronted Jack. He told me it was the first time he had been on the site for a long time and that he was just seeing how many messages he had received up until then. He claimed he needed to clear out his mailbox, which he did. I asked him why any of that even mattered to him and his explanation was that because his membership was soon expiring, he just wanted everything cleared out. He assured me that I was the love of his life and he didn't need or want anyone else. His level of sincerity convinced me. I was a happy girl again.

About a month later, Jack and I made mad passionate love on board his boat one morning and afterwards, I took a quick shower before we were went ashore for breakfast. As I was changing in the stateroom I assumed Jack was on the upper deck playing with his boating instruments, but I had a suspicion that came over me. I wanted to prove my instinct wrong. I REALLY wanted to prove myself wrong so I went to my phone and pulled the site up. I saw that he was not only still active on the site but was online at that very moment. I couldn't believe it. We had just made love for two hours, but he still had some need to connect with another woman. I was livid. I just didn't know what to do. I could simply pack up and split in a huff or I could wait a while and disappear when he wasn't around. I chose the latter. I didn't want a confrontation. I didn't want any more lies. And I further saw that he didn't let his membership expire, but was probably paid up for another six months.

I left Jack later that day. I nicely graced him by leaving behind a note that said I needed to be with someone who enjoyed my company and was happy dating one woman at a time. I felt I couldn't trust him anymore and that he had ruined a good thing. I told him there was no need to call me anymore and I ended the message with "Goodbye my friend, Jill." I liked the drama of my closing remark.

Jack did call repeatedly after that, but I never responded. And I've decided to stay off the site for a few months. As a matter of fact, since my membership expired months ago, I may never go back on but I will presume the unfaithful jerk is still going on it and climbing the online dating hill with his bucket of water. It's a crying shame that Jack made that second cheating mistake with me because this Jill isn't tumbling down any more. He won't find another loving and caring girl like me again, or at least anytime soon. I guarantee it.

Take-Away: *The old saying you don't realize what you have until you don't have it anymore applies here. Also, the grass isn't always greener on the other side. When you find a good apple keep it, and quit looking for a better one.*

Do You Take Checks?

I met a nice guy on a site called *Seeking Arrangement*. We had been instant messaging back and forth for several weeks and decided to get together. Since I lived in Naples, Florida and he was in New York City, he offered to fly down to see me.

As I was new on this particular site, a friend of mine who was experienced with its protocols gave me some advice on how to handle the weekend arrangements. She said that I needed to have my date make reservations at a hotel in Naples because it wasn't cool to invite a complete stranger to spend the weekend at my house. Paul was fine with that and booked a room at a great beachside resort for the following weekend. My friend also advised me to clarify his financial intentions and expectations. He and I negotiated a $1,000 allowance per day for the three days he'd be with me. There was no sex promised.

I had in mind some restaurants and activities for our weekend itinerary and because Naples was my home turf, it was easy to list all my personal picks of choice. It just so happened that his visit was falling on a holiday weekend, President's Day, which I knew to be a terrific time for special sales and events at Waterside, my favorite shopping venue. Hermes, Louis Vuitton and Tiffany's are all there. So, I'm figuring, in addition to the agreed allowance, maybe I could get Paul to take me for a shopping trip there, an extra little perk for me. I decided I would play it by ear on all my other ideas once Paul arrived.

Paul showed up as planned and I met him for drinks and dinner the first night. He was as handsome as his pictures and charming as I had expected. We ate at the hotel where he was staying, which boasts an amazing restaurant called Baleen and is situated directly on the beach. After a couple bottles of champagne, we decided it would be risky for me to drive home so I spent the night with him at the resort. The weather next day turned out to be gorgeous and we ended up spending the entire weekend either in his room or at the beach. I had no complaints whatsoever, although we never did make it to Waterside for shopping. I figured I would take my allowance money and go shopping for myself after he left.

As we were going down for lunch on Monday, the last day of his visit, Paul said he needed to stop at his bank to get some cash. I assumed the cash was to pay me my allowance for the weekend. He asked if there was a Citibank nearby. I knew of a branch on Third Street.

We had a nice brunch and by then it was 2 p.m. Since Paul's flight departed at 4:10, time was pressing. Because I had offered to drive him to the airport myself so he could catch the bank, I went with him back to his room to get his suitcase. We squeezed in a last minute quickie before closing the door and dashed to the lobby for checkout. I summoned the valet for my car and we were off for the airport.

When I pulled into a spot at the bank, I noticed the parking lot was empty. *What's up with that?* I wondered as Paul headed for the front door. He came back a few minutes later and informed me that the bank was closed. It was President's Day. I couldn't believe it, but Paul told me not to worry as he reached into his carryon and pulled out his checkbook. He quickly wrote out a check and handed it to me. I expected it to be for $3,000 but it was made out for $3,500 instead. My charming Paul then told me that he had an amazing time and was looking forward to spending a lot more time with me. I felt funny taking the check. As a matter of fact, those moments in the car felt really awkward, so I quickly stuck the check in my console to get it out of sight and skipped to the subject of making it to the airport on time.

Once we arrived at the drop off curb, we hugged and kissed goodbye. Paul told me that he would call during the week, but that he was going to be out of town the following weekend on business. We made tentative plans for the weekend after in New York. I drove away thinking it had been a successful date, well worth it. Paul texted that night and thanked me again for a great weekend. I texted back with a smiley icon saying, "It was my pleasure."

The next day I deposited my check.

On Thursday I checked the balance in my checking account and that's when I learned that Paul's check had bounced. I was horrified. I called him right away and he assured me the check was good and that I should redeposit it. I did, but on Monday I got notice that the check was drawn on an account that had been closed. I can't begin to describe how I was feeling.

I called Paul, but only got his voicemail. I frantically texted him with a demand that he make the check good or else. He didn't respond. I probably called him a hundred more times over the following days, but to no avail. The lying bum had duped me and then dumped me on top of it. My good friend insisted I should have him arrested for passing a bad check, but I never did. It was all just too humiliating and upsetting to go there. I was definitely used and taken advantage of.

I'll NEVER go online seeking arrangements again!

Take-Away: There are so many con-artists in real life and especially on the internet. Make sure you get paid up front if you have an arrangement. That includes flights, hotel rooms and when appropriate, your time. Very rarely will you ever get paid when a date goes badly, and as you can see from the above, you can even get burnt when the date goes well. Don't trust right away. Trust must be earned, and it takes more than the first meeting.

Payback Is A Bitch

This is a story about an ugly divorce. In order to finalize the miserable court battle, Peter gave his ex- wife a hefty settlement that included an outrageous amount of child and spousal support. He then decided to get back at his former spouse using the internet.

He went to a website that specialized in connecting couples for mutually agreeable "arrangements," the jest of it intended to be more long term in nature and not at all typical of the usual online dating sites. You might say women who posted there were looking to become a guy's special girlfriend, mistress, lover or friend. The site was set up to input photographs and a detailed profile, as well as the desired amount of money to be paid as part of the arrangement.

So Peter went to work setting up a post on behalf of his former wife, unbeknownst to her. In the profile he created were sexually explicit personal qualities that would appeal to men. He even uploaded nude pictures of her in the "special" section where he could control viewing access of them by any interested men. He answered all the questions describing what she was looking for in an arrangement, noting her desire to continue living in the style she had become accustomed. The desired amount of money requested was $10,000 and $20,000 a month. The juicier part of her post was that she would perform any sexual favors for her partner and that she was completely uninhibited with her sexuality. The latter was intended to infer her interest in either a male or female partner, swinging with multiple partners or whatever one's imagination might fathom.

Peter then set up a separate email account with the name *Pamthepleaser*. When the online inquiries began coming in, Peter answered back on this private email address as if he was Pam. He was getting a lot of interested men on the hook and responded to each with erotic details of what she, *Pamthepleaser*, would do for the right amount of money. Between the naked pictures and the raw email responses, Peter was making Pam look like the biggest whore in town.

It wasn't until a guy recognized Pam in a department store one day, from having seen her photos online, and what he thought of was their sexy online conversations. He approached her, introducing himself with the notion she'd know who he was from the website. She didn't, of course, but he was certain he was not mistaken about her identity and persisted in verbally strong-arming her for a dinner date. When she became insulted by his aggressive approach and started to walk away, he threatened to have her blacklisted from their website…that got her attention.

Pam went home emotionally drained from the encounter, and after researching the site the guy had mentioned became horrified to discover her photo there with the descriptive profile. She called her friend, sobbing hysterically, and together they went to the police to report the obvious internet identity theft.

A sting operation was set up to catch the culprit and Paul was busted. Pam pressed charges and because the evidence produced from the sting was concrete proof against him, he pled guilty.

Although he didn't get jail time he now has a criminal record. Reports are that he will be registered as a sexual predator, too.

Take-Away: It's never easy getting over an ex. You'll always have feelings for them, whether good or bad. But if it's the latter, don't do anything that you may come to regret in the future. Think first of the consequences of your actions. Hopefully you'll think clearly and redirect your anger elsewhere in a more positive direction.

Home Shopping

Imagine dating a man for eight months who you met online. And imagine that you met him on the *Seeking Arrangement* website and he was helping you that whole time to pay your bills. Imagine that you were really falling in love with him. That's not imaginary for me. It's the truth of my situation.

Rob was smart, funny and extremely good looking. I would see him at least twice a week and sometimes more. He had been going through an ugly divorce and had two children who he saw on the weekends. Otherwise, he was a workaholic in the real estate business. I had the impression he was doing well financially because he drove a large BMW and was paying for the lease on my BMW as well. He was honestly the ideal boyfriend. I couldn't have asked for someone more caring, romantic and sexual. He was probably the best lover I've ever had.

One night Rob surprised me. He told me that although he wasn't ready to get married again after his terrible divorce that he thought we should move in together. He also said he thought it was a good time to buy real estate as the economy was improving and maybe if we found the right house, we should look for one to call our own. I was so happy that he wanted to take our relationship to the next level. I told him I would love to find a house to share with him. He suggested that I start looking around.

The following week I started my home search. I looked through magazines and newspaper. I circled ads in the newspaper for houses that looked interesting and were held open on Sundays. I spent countless Sunday afternoons looking for a great home for us, and after a couple of months had narrowed my search down to three. Since Rob was in the business, he called the listing agents of the homes and made an appointment for the following Wednesday afternoon, his day off, to look at the homes with me. Of the three, there was one that Rob really fell in love with. We had similar tastes. It happened to be my favorite too. It was a Mediterranean home with four bedrooms, an open kitchen and Florida room, four bathrooms and a three car garage. There was a generous backyard with a gorgeous pool and spa with a built in barbeque area. It was really magnificent and the best part was that it was never lived in before. Apparently the owner had run into financial problems and it was offered for sale almost $200,000 under market value as a "short" sale. I didn't really know what that type of sale meant so Rob explained. It is a situation where the mortgage on the property was actually more than the asking price. The bank was willing to take less money than what was owed in order to sell the place quickly. Rob explained that the process was quite commonplace and although it took a long time to actually close on the home, it would be well worth the wait in the long run. The deal seemed incredible. I felt certain Rob knew what he was doing.

After three months passed, Rob told me that we didn't get the house. He said the bank had rejected our offer and it appeared they had received a higher bid from someone else. I was disappointed, to say the least, as my dream home with my dream man would have to be put on hold until we found another one.

Rob and I continued to date, but it wasn't near as often anymore. I was only seeing him once a week. The other thing that I noticed was that he never brought up the house subject again. When I asked him if there was something wrong he said, "No, honey. Of course not. I'm just busier at work right now. It's my busy season, but we're cool." I never brought up the house search again as I figured he would when he was ready.

One afternoon I happened to be driving past the home that Rob and I previously tried to buy. I noticed that the new owners had moved in. There was a car in the driveway, more landscaping in the front yard and even a swing set on the side of the house. I envied the people who had moved in. They were lucky to have such a nice place and I felt sad that Rob and I hadn't gotten it. Had we, I would have been seeing my man every day instead of only once a week now. He seemed to be getting even more distant from me as the days passed.

Then one night Rob gave me some bad news. He told me that he was getting back with his wife. He told me that he really wanted to be with his kids more and that for the good of the kids, it was important that he try to make his marriage to their mother work. I was devastated. He told me that he would continue to help me pay my bills for several more months, but that he wouldn't be able to see me any longer. I can't begin to say how hurt I felt. I had really fallen for him and imagined us sharing a future together. I cried for a whole week and my life seemed to be coming apart.

It had been about a month since the last time I saw Rob and I don't know what possessed me, but I had the urge to drive past the house he and I almost shared together. Slowly I turned the corner onto the street and wallowed in my "what if" thoughts. What if the sale could have occurred more quickly, would he and I still be together? What if I had just worked at the house search more diligently, would moving in together have saved our relationship? I was really working myself into having another heartbroken day until I came into view of the home.

Parked in the driveway was a car just like Rob's. At first I pitifully thought, "What a cruel coincidence." I slowed down from 10 mph to about 2 mph and looked closer just as I was beginning to tear up and pass by the driveway entrance. Wait a minute. I stomped my foot on the brakes. That car had Rob's license plate. I came to a dead stop in the middle of the street and everything started to register as I began to speculate on the past events. There were a million questions racing through my head. Did he in fact buy the house from the bank but didn't tell me? Did that bastard end up buying our house after our breakup? Did he have me pick out the house so he could go back to his family in a new home? Was he even going through a divorce during the months we were dating? Did I essentially pick out the house for him and his family? Are they living in my f….. house? I was working myself into a complete rage.

I didn't know what to do with all the anger building up in me. I wanted to pull right into the driveway and confront him then and there. I was so angry that I wanted to smash into his car at sixty miles per hour. I seriously might have done just that had I not had the presence to remember he was still paying for the lease on mine. I'd be cutting my own nose off if I wrecked both his car and mine. But then, under the circumstances, why should I care about being rational. It was looking pretty obvious that he had screwed me over royally. But wait. Maybe I should be sure of what he did before jumping to conclusions so I raced back home and went to the computer. I looked up the property address on the tax website to see who owned the property. Sure enough, the house was in his wife's name. "You bastard!" I screamed out aloud several times or more. I didn't even care if any of my neighbors heard me. I realized the SOB made me find them a house to live in and he was probably never getting divorced either. *That f..... liar!*

I called his cell phone. He didn't pick up. He knew it was me. I left him a scathing voicemail that I probably shouldn't have, but I didn't care at that moment. It was not very ladylike. I used language that my mama wouldn't be proud of coming from the mouth of her little girl. Then I finished my rant by saying he'd better call me back soon or else I'd be coming over to his new house to break it in for him. Pretty threatening, huh? I didn't even know what I meant by that, but the obvious would have been to tell his wife about our relationship, in case she didn't already know about it, and that I would do everything in my power to get even with him.

Rob did call back later that day. He insisted that he didn't lie to me. He said he was going through the divorce like he said until he realized that he should try for the sake of his children to make it work. He told me all about the house and that the bank reconsidered his offer later when the other buyer failed to close on the deal. He said it was too good of a deal for him not to go ahead and buy it. He promised he would never have had me pick out a house for the two of us with the intention of moving his family into it. "What kind of a guy do you think I am?" he asked.

I didn't answer with what I was thinking, especially because he told me he intended to continue paying my car lease payments for the duration of the lease. He knew that gesture wouldn't alleviate my pain and heartache, but probably hoped it would make things a little easier for me and I wouldn't go to my grave someday still thinking he was a complete ass.

My Rob turned out to be a real creep and I'm still not sure that I believe one bit of his story about the bank and the house. My girlfriends told me that Rob wasn't the only married guy on this website and that whatever I went through with Rob, there were probably hundreds of other girls who have been hurt and used the way I was.

Take-Away: Ladies, there are so many married men on these sites. Don't ever expect a happy ending from a married man, no matter what he promises you. It's one of the oldest stories known to man.

Tony or Tonya?

Let me introduce myself. I am a guy. I am a guy who loves women because they are soft, pretty to look at and smell divine with all their perfumes and cosmetics. To me, they are a heavenly creation and even at my age of maturity, I am still quite honestly awestruck by them.

So I met this girl online, an especially pretty girl of color. What attracted me most though was that she had the largest chest I've ever seen. Her photos highlighted those breasts the way an arrow sign and flashing neon lights would command your attention. As a matter of fact, one picture of her left me imagining that there was a subliminal "Welcome" sign hung around her neck.

Our first date was for dinner at Mario's Restaurant. Upon greeting her at the bar that evening, I was somewhat intimated to see that she was about six feet tall. She had impeccable posture, the perfect weight for her size, big boned and athletic (petite is more my preference, but that really doesn't have a thing to do with this story). Tonya was wearing a skin-tight dress that was very low cut in the front and so short that it barely covered her hoochie-coo. Save me!

We were seated outside for cocktails, and were having a pleasant conversation when she told me that she was into fortune telling. She explained that she had the gift of palm reading and asked if I wanted her to give me a reading. Being the sport that I am, I extended my hand. She clasped my wrist with her left hand and laid my hand gently into her right. Now I have what would be considered bigger-than-average size hands for a guy, but HER hands were so big they made mine look dwarfed by comparison. As I sat listening to her reading I began to wonder, *How can a girl have bigger hands than me? Could Tonya be a guy?*

Throughout the rest of our dinner, my mind was uneasy pondering that question so I wrapped the evening up as quickly as politely possible. I was so uncomfortable with the idea I was having a dinner date with a guy, albeit a very chesty guy with a great shape, that I couldn't bring myself to return text messages the next day from Tonya. Suspect too, I realized, was her name. Tonya is pretty close to the name Tony, right? Talk about naïve.

Take-Away: It is getting much more difficult to tell anymore as surgeries are being perfected. When in doubt, look for the Adams apple. Even that can be removed nowadays. A real dilemma; although, big hands and big feet and deeper voice are still the early warning signs of choice.

Who Let The Dog Out

I met a girl online who shared lots in common with me. The main thing was that we were both dog lovers, and more specifically we both had a passion for rescue dogs. I had always believed that any woman who rescued dogs had to have a kind heart and be a loving person. I also have a deep affection for women who are nurses for the same reason. It's a special person who enjoys helping people (and animals), and this personality trait is high on my list.

Heather was not only kind hearted and loving, she was beautiful. She had brown hair with sexy green eyes and a body to die for, and that sealed the deal for me. On our first date we went out for dinner in a busy downtown area known as Cityplace. We had lots to talk about and I told her about losing my rescue terrier just two months earlier. She told me about her newest adoption, a mixed-breed boxer named Simon. It just so happened that both of us were in the real estate business and knew many of the same people. Also, we both loved to travel and had the same favorite places in Europe. At this point it seemed that we were a match made in heaven. After dinner we took a hand-held walk while window shopping, and when the evening was drawing to a close, she invited me to her place. She was comfortable with me and since she lived nearby, we just strolled on to her house. She wanted me to meet Simon.

When we got to her place, her boxer named Simon came running to the door immediately. He was big and had what to me looked like a mean glare in his eye when I stepped in the door. He wearily backed away before I had the chance to give him my hand. He cowered on his doggie bed on the front room floor, tail tucked, and continued eyeing me cautiously as I sat down on the couch. He didn't growl, but was definitely leery of my presence. Since I loved dogs and thought I was a pretty experienced dog handler, I determined I could make friends with him. Heather gave me a bone to give him and he took it promptly when I offered it, but took it back to his bed to chew. That seemed to ease his tension and I figured he was going to warm up to me little by little now. I always knew that I was an acquired taste!

When Heather got up to go to the kitchen, I thought Simon might be less protective of his master and give me an opportunity to become his friend. So I got up from the couch and gently approached him. I squatted down and held out my hand. He cautiously sniffed. I then reached to pet the top of his gigantic head but didn't quite get there before he snapped. With alligator speed, he clamped down on my hand. It happened so fast I had no time to pull back. He bit and released immediately. It wasn't vicious, just a snap but I knew his canines had punctured deep and blood immediately began dripping from the wounds in the meat of my hand. I vaguely remember hearing myself sort of yelp when it happened and that brought Heather running from the kitchen. She looked at me standing beside Simon with blood streaming from my dangling arm and I thought she was going to faint. I thought I was going to faint, but neither of us did. She grabbed a towel and we wrapped my hand. I wasn't really sure how badly I was hurt, but knew it was hurting terribly and now bleeding profusely. I was thankful that my hand was still attached to my arm.

Heather called 911 and the paramedics arrived within minutes. They took me to the hospital where I was given two shots, one for rabies and the other to numb my hand so they could stitch the gash. Two hours and twenty-four stitches later, we left the hospital.

Heather couldn't apologize enough. She kept blaming herself and of course I assured her it wasn't her fault at all. I understood that the dog didn't know me and was frightfully insecure about my intentions under the circumstances. He felt cornered in his bed and was scared. It was really a mistake on my part.

She cradled my hand lovingly, it now being wrapped up like a boxer's hand before a heavyweight fight. I tried to make light of the incident by referring to her two boxers, Simon the dog and me, but she cried anyway. Her tears were still flowing as she drove me back to my car that night and, although I think I was lucky in retrospect to still have all five fingers in tack, those tears of hers took my mind off my throbbing hand for awhile. I felt bad for her.

I only saw Heather once for coffee after that, and she continued to call me every day for a couple of weeks to check on me, but I think we both realized that a relationship probably wasn't in the cards since I was never going to be Simon's friend. I didn't want to risk becoming his dinner next time. I never saw Heather or Simon again.

No Class In First Class

I met a guy on a travel dating site. Charlie was from the Fort Lauderdale, Florida area, which is just up the highway from Miami where I live. He and I had several favorite destinations in common so we had plenty to talk about. Aside from Greece and Italy, we both loved Rome, not because either of us were Catholic but because of the antiquities all over the place and its history. One big difference between us though was age. I was thirty-six and he was forty years my senior.

From our phone conversations, I found Charlie to be a really fun person. He was smart as a whip and kept me in stitches with his funny quips and quotes that he would interject when I least expected it. He was good at keeping me on my toes because I never knew when he'd throw something out from left field to stump me. It would be fair to say he enjoyed being a bit of a prankster.

Charlie thought we should make our first trip together a fun trip. He recommended Las Vegas and told me poker stories from times he'd been there. He said he had played with the big boys a few times and promised to wear a diamond ring he was given after winning a tournament at Harrah's many years ago. I asked him if he still played and he said no, but I started thinking he might have been underplaying the truth of that.

I agreed to go to Las Vegas with him and he made all the arrangements for our weekend getaway. I met him at the airport on a Thursday night. He greeted me with a big bear hug and we checked our bags for the flight. Once through security and down the hallway to our gate, Charlie then handed me my ticket and told me we wouldn't be sitting together. I was very surprised. He explained the reason was because his ticket had been paid for by the casino and had been sent separately; therefore he wasn't able to get us seats together, hard as he tried. I told him it was okay and not a big deal. It was a big deal.

What happened next is what made the small deal into a big deal with me. When the steward began boarding our flight, he first called for all first class passengers. Charlie got up and said, "I guess that's me."

That's when it dawned on me. Not only were we NOT sitting together, but we weren't even in the same section. He was flying first class and the cheap bastard had me sitting in economy. I couldn't believe it. I was so angered that I didn't even want to go on the trip with this poker-playing, old guy. If I could have retrieved my bags off the plane, I would have left the airport pronto and never looked back, but I didn't.

I made the best of the trip and ate marvelously well while there. Our suite had two separate bedrooms with amazing views of the Strip and I did appreciate that aspect of the weekend. I couldn't help imagine though what my accommodations might have been if Casino Charlie hadn't been given the suite. I think he was fairly frustrated with me for giving a cold shoulder when he tried getting intimate a time or two. Nope. I had several hours during my economy flight to make that decision, and sleeping with him was not even on my radar screen. I politely lied as a gesture of kindness and told him it was my time of the month. I could tell he was disappointed, but I wanted no part of him after the weekend. So much for that high roller!

Take-Away: *You can't teach an old dog new tricks. You can't teach class to a person with no class. Be realistic in your expectations and maybe dating a much older guy is not always the answer. Sorry Charlie.*

Sight For Sore Eyes

I met George on the internet and became better acquainted with him over several weeks via Skype. I thought it was very cool to communicate that way so there wouldn't be any big surprises when we actually met, especially because he was considerably older than me. He was good looking and from what I could see appeared to be in pretty good shape. When he told me he had booked a trip for us to the Bahamas, I was thrilled. He told me to pack light and added, "Lite, like my beer." I could tell he was excited about the trip too.

We met up in Nassau because he was coming from Chicago and I was in Florida. My flight landed an hour before his and I waited for him at his arriving gate. I recognized him immediately as he came walking down the corridor. Everything was good at this point, but got even better when our taxi delivered us to the Atlantis Hotel on Paradise Island. It was just gorgeous and our room had a wonderful balcony overlooking the ocean. I was jazzed and could hardly wait to get into my bathing suit so George and I could scout the pools and beaches below.

I put on my cute bikini and when I came out of the bathroom, George was in his swimsuit and swinging two beach towels around over his head with a big old smile on his face. "Surf's up, babe. Wanna hula dance?"

That's when everything went downhill for me. I could have overlooked the fact that he was one of the hairiest men I had ever seen or that he had a twenty-pound donut of blubber around his midsection, but his complete absence of shame and embarrassment over his absurd appearance hailed brimstones on my Caribbean joy. His swimsuit was smaller than my itsy-bitsy, teeny-weeny yellow polka dot bikini. It was a sea turtle green Speedo that was lost under his belly and from the front looked as if he had nothing on at all. I only wish I could erase from memory the site of his hairy buns. He had a butt-crack that was totally magnified due to the roundness of the hairy twins. He looked ridiculous!

If I had known him better I would have said, "No. No. No. You can't wear that in public!" I held my tongue.

Our weekend went by quickly and even as nice of a guy as George was and as hard as he tried to make our trip a romantic getaway, it just didn't go that way. It was more of a friendship than anything else.

I don't know what to recommend to someone else who is looking for a travel mate on this site. Even with Skype, there's no way to know what's under the clothing, and even if you could know ahead of time what's hidden from view, how would you know if the guy sports a Speedo?

After my weekend with George, I learned an important lesson. That WILL be one of the first questions I ask from now on.

Take-Away: Guys, unless you're on the Olympic Swim Team, an underwear model with Calvin Klein, or speak Italian fluently, you have no business wearing a Speedo. A real turn-off for most women.

Cruise To Nowhere Nightmare

I met Vicky online and it seemed like we were a great match. We both loved to travel; we both loved dining out; we're both close to our families; we're both recently divorced and neither of us have kids. So right off the bat, we had a lot in common.

The first time we met was at a pub in the city. It was after work in the middle of the week and we had a blast together talking and laughing with the locals there. It reminded me of the old television series "Cheers". Our second date was more quiet and romantic at a little Italian bistro. In both settings, Vicky was comfortable and very enjoyable to be with. We kissed goodnight on both occasions and I felt a strong physical chemistry was in the making!

It just so happened that the following week I noticed an email from a cruise company advertising a "Cruise to Nowhere" the upcoming weekend. The ship was to disembark on Friday night and return early Monday morning from a port that was convenient to both Vicky and me. The schedule would fit both of our work schedules too, and it was bargain priced for last minute travelers. So I called the reservation number to ask the sales agent to explain the "catch" for the very cheap price. She promised there were no catches to it and that they simply offered the special pricing in order to fill the last few empty cabins to have full capacity on board. She assured me that it was an all-inclusive cruise, and defined that to mean all meals, entertainment and non-stop fun were included in the price. She also explained that the price did not include drinks, tips and port charges. She said I would have to commit quickly if I wanted to secure a cabin.

I called Vicky and asked if she was interested in going. With not a bit of hesitation, she accepted my invitation and I booked the cruise. Later that night we talked and began to imagine how much fun it was going to be sitting poolside, kicking back with cocktails and taking in all the ship's entertainment. We were both excited about the trip, and I thought to myself it was the perfect setting to consummate our relationship. Who wouldn't find it romantic to be on a beautiful ship at sea feeling warm ocean breezes over azure blue water and dreamy starlit nights?

Friday finally arrived and sad to say, it was raining the whole day. As a matter of fact, it was such a wet day that mist hung heavily in the air. Even when the rain finally let up, the gray mist was so thick that water dripped from everything making a soggy mess. Visibility was very limited. But as evening approached and I arrived at the dock to meet Vicky, there was a small break in the weather. The cloud cover opened up just as Vicky appeared at the gangway and a magnificent ray of sunshine was cast over the pier making our kiss and hug greeting something of a magical moment. We were giddy with excitement.

After checking in, I followed behind Vicky as we were escorted down the elevator and along the hallway toward our cabin. I couldn't wait to spend the next few days with her. She looked hot as heck wearing some tight jeans and a belly shirt. Her perfume lingered in the air and I savored the fragrance with anticipation. We were like two little kids, both excited to be not only on our first cruise ever but to be experiencing it together.

When the porter opened the door to our cabin, Vicky and I were in disbelief. It was a jaw-dropping, eye-popping moment. In front of us was the smallest room we had ever seen in our lives. It was more like a closet than a room and yet more shocking than that was the sight of bunk beds. Yes, you heard right, not a single, double, queen nor king but bunk beds. They were bunk beds, real bunk beds like the kind children sleep on. And did I mention, there were no windows in the place?

"No. No. No. This is not acceptable. Not acceptable."

The porter did his best to explain there were no other options as the ship was completely full. I wanted to throw a giant temper tantrum, but held off not wanting to make a bad scene in front of Vicky. I turned to Vicky and said, "Do you still want to do this? It's not too late to go back."

Vicky looked pretty sad but said, "Of course not. We'll make this work. Besides if you think about it, just how much time are we going to spend in the room anyway? We're only going to be in here to dress and sleep. We'll be at the pool and on deck most of the trip."

I liked her attitude and agreed to take the cabin, but my disappointment with the accommodations put a damper on my mood. However, I pulled myself together and decided to focus more positively on enjoying the weekend with my lady, no matter what the conditions. We were going to make the best of things.

First we went to the deck for the lifeboat drill and walked around the ship. The pool, dining room, fitness and spa facilities looked pretty nice. We then returned to the cabin to dress for dinner, and that was when I first saw our bathroom. It was so tiny and under other circumstances, I would have laughed over it thinking it had to be a joke, but it wasn't. The sink was the size of a medium salad bowl and the commode was obviously made for a six year old child. The shower stall was compactly designed for perpendicular standing only. If you dropped your bar of soap, I have no idea how you'd ever get to it since there was no room to bend over! Did I mention too that the water pressure was practically non- existent? I felt slightly claustrophobic with the whole thing. The bunk beds, the closet-cabin and now the miniature bathroom were weighing heavily on me. Vicky could tell I wasn't a happy camper, but she kept her sense of humor; I was rapidly losing mine.

Off to dinner we went and had mediocre food, saw a mediocre show in a mediocre theater and the only laugh of the evening came when we returned to our cabin with the bunk beds and Vicky asked me if I liked being on top? We both laughed over the obvious sexual inference. I climbed up on the top bunk, being the gentleman I always try to be, and fell fast asleep, exhausted from my state of agitation.

The following day, I woke up and the room was pitch black. I checked my watch to see it was 9:00 a.m. Vicky was still asleep. I thought to myself, *Stay positive. It's a new day. Things will get better.* I slipped out of the top bunk in my boxers and looked down the hallway. It was dark. No one was in sight so I headed toward the double doors that led to a deck and peeked out. I wanted to cry. It was pouring down rain.

The weekend turned out to be a raining, miserable disaster. I couldn't shake my crummy mood no matter how I tried. We spent three whole nights in that "closet" together and never consummated our relationship. The rain was relentless to the bitter end of the cruise and what should have been a romantic frolic was an unfortunate fiasco. Romance didn't have a fighting chance under the circumstances.

Although Vicky and I talked the week after our cruise, we never saw each other again. So much for the love boat!

Take-Away: *If a deal seems too good to be true, it usually is. Expect the worst and do your due diligence before it's too late to do anything about it.*

Dirty Girl

If you've never seen the YouTube video of the now-famous girl who loved cats, you may not fully appreciate my internet dating story about another girl who loved cats. Her name was Heidi and what a cute gal, cute like the actress Katherine Heigl. Honestly, Heidi had blonde hair, perfectly petite body, beautiful complexion and a personality as cute as her face. The first time I met her in person, I was captivated and thought to myself *This is THE ONE!*

Our first date ended with a little kiss, and I was excited waiting for the following Friday to see her again. She met me for coffee at the Coffee Bean that night and from there we walked along the boardwalk at sunset. We then had a romantic dinner at a seafood restaurant known for its delicious mussels, served in about twenty different ways. Excellent wine, bread, mussels, and conversation left me convinced I had finally hooked a "keeper". As a matter of fact, I found myself thinking about how my mom would just adore this girl and imagined her fitting into my family terrifically.

Heidi surprised me the next day with an invitation to her condo for a home cooked dinner and a movie the following Friday night. She asked me to pick up a couple of DVDs, my choice, and she would take care of dinner and dessert. This was beginning to look like heaven raining down blessings on this dog of a bachelor. She was nesting, luring me in with home cooked food! Just when I thought I was going to have to try with all my might to catch her, she was trying to catch me using that old trick, "The way to a man's heart is through his stomach."

To this point, I had learned a lot about Heidi during our conversations. She was thirty-two and had never been married, although had been in what she considered being two significant relationships during her life. She worked as a doctor's assistant and was well paid for a job that she felt was a fulfilling occupation. Secretly, I imagined it would be great to have a wife who would be my personal nurse. She had a close and loving relationship with her parents and two younger siblings who lived in Braxton, a town forty-five minutes away and I liked that because they were close, but not too close. She drove a beautiful new Lexus, too, which just so happened to be the exact color and model I had thought of buying recently. The whole package seemed too good to be true. She loved to travel and her favorite activity was snow skiing. When we talked about our travel bucket list, there were eight of ten places we both longed to visit and they were specific, like not just the country of India, but Bombay specifically.

We both chose Telluride as our favorite place to snow ski. She also said she was a cat lover, but not being at all partial to cats myself, I just pretty much ignored that subject. I was convinced we were the perfect match for a lifelong relationship and after knowing each other only two weeks with two dates, I tell you the truth, I was ready to propose!

Further, Heidi was hot. Our eyes had met in ways that put a flame torch in my man parts if you get my drift! So, as I anticipated our dinner and movie date at her condo that Friday night, you can guess where my mind had been all day.

With fresh flowers in hand and DVDs in the other, I rang her doorbell at exactly 7 p.m. The door opened and there she was to greet me, but OMG! There was the most terrible odor the minute she opened the door and when I stepped inside, it was even worse. Suddenly at my feet were four cats, all purring and snaking their tails around my pant legs. Heidi was making the biggest fuss over them, introducing them each by name and I could have cared less!

With a little peck on my cheek, she thanked me for the flowers and told me to make myself at home with her babies while she took care of some things in the kitchen for a minute. I was speechless when she picked Fred up and put him in my arms, cat dander and hair flying into the air as she showed me how to caress him just right. She ogled over the disgusting feline creature, kissing it repeatedly. She disappeared into the kitchen and I wanted to put a face mask over my mouth and nose.

"Make myself at home?"

I was freaking out. There were four litter boxes, two at each end of her couch. There were magazines and newspaper strewn across the floor and stacked everywhere. Even in the dimly lit room, I could see her clothes draped over every piece of furniture in the place, including the dress she had worn the prior week on our date. Two empty soda cans and some candy wrappers covered the coffee table and worse than that was a leftover plate of spaghetti. I had to move her laptop and a bowl of dried cat food to find a place to sit on the filthy, cat-hair-covered couch. And worse yet, a pillow at the far end of the couch looked like it had a big damp spot, so I sat as far from it as possible. This was NOT Katherine Heigl. This was Heidi, the dirty girl who had four cats and lived in a stinking, dirty condo,

I did eat the dinner, watched the movies and had a little romance that night, but knew in my heart this relationship was never going to work.

Diaper Dan

You've probably heard the name Dapper Dan before. When I looked up the meaning of the word dapper its definition was "fit, groomed and attractive." The only reference I found for both words together as a name was relating to a racehorse back in the 1960's who was named Dapper Dan. He came close to winning the Kentucky Derby and was viewed as being one of the most attractive and well-groomed racehorses of the time, thus our common use of his name for certain people who fit the same description.

I mention this because I recently met someone online by the name of Dan. He was about my age, middle forties, and was a good looking, fit guy. We went out a couple of times and always had fun. One night he called and asked me if I liked Bruce Springsteen. I replied, "Who doesn't? He's The Boss!" He then said he had a chance to get concert tickets and asked if I would like to go with him. I jumped on the invitation to revisit my younger days of rock.

Three weeks later Dan and I were on our way to the concert. I couldn't wait to see Springsteen live. As a matter of fact, I pulled out my old Springsteen albums to show Dan. I could tell he was green with envy, and we talked about the early days. I told him I had always heard his live shows were long, three hours or more and he said he'd heard the same thing. It was fun going down memory lane with him as we drove to the venue for the show that night. It was good to be with him and to be going to see Springsteen too. We were a good match as a couple.

When we were in the line of cars slowly getting parked in the stadium lot, Dan told me he had two things he wanted to tell me before we got into the crowd of people. He said he liked me a lot and that he didn't want me to think he was weird by telling me the two things. From his tone of voice, I wasn't sure I wanted to know. Who wants bad news right before a Springsteen concert? But I told him to go ahead. First, he confessed that he loved to smoke marijuana. He then handed me a tin Altoids container, which I opened and saw rolled joints in it. There was a moment of silence, but then I smiled and said I'd join him. He then said the second thing he wanted to say might really seem weird to me, but I assured him it was okay by me to go ahead. He said, "You know The Boss wouldn't like someone in the audience getting up during the long show to go to the bathroom, so here it comes. I'm wearing adult diapers under my pants."

"What?"

"I'm wearing diapers so I don't have to miss a minute of the show." He then pulled up his shirt tail to show me the paper and plastic diaper down the front of his pants.

"Dan," I said. "I've never heard of anyone doing that. I mean, if you went to the bathroom like a normal person during the show during a new song or less popular one, wouldn't that make better sense than peeing in your pants?"

I could see nothing I was going to say would change his intentions. He loved all of Springsteen's songs and wasn't going to miss one minute of the event whether I liked it or not. I insisted the diapers were made for adults and that made it not weird, but I found the whole thing disgusting. I made him promise he wouldn't tell me when he was doing it or it might ruin the whole concert for me.

"I don't want to know," I insisted. "It'll totally freak me out."

The concert lasted way over three hours. It was amazing and The Boss is definitely the best entertainer I've ever seen perform live. As far as Dan's diaper went, he assured me afterwards that he only went number one just once. When we were walking back to the car he even said, "I'd never poop in them." That comment just made the whole thing even more disgusting, as if that made the whole thing fine? I was grossed out with him the whole way home and swear I could smell urine. I think it might have dripped down his pant leg, so I purposely avoided even looking his way.

I realize nobody is perfect and everybody has baggage they carry around, but I'm afraid a boyfriend with a dirty diaper bag isn't for me. He was once my Dapper Dan but now I'll refer to him as Diaper Dan. I never went out with him again.

On Pins And Needles

People who know me would say I am gutsy and independent. I am. As a professional female in a male dominated career field, I've learned how to stand my ground when playing ball with the big boys. There is little that can trip my trigger because I've learned to remain unmoved no matter what pitch they throw at me.

But when I turned thirty-five, I decided it was time to find Mr. Right. Since my career had dominated my life up to then, it was with purposeful intent that I signed up with an internet dating site. My goal was to make up for lost time in the world of romance. I rigorously read and reviewed bios of single men and found one that sounded like my perfect match. I immediately honed in on Mr. Right and scheduled a dinner date.

We met at Bonefish Grill and I was delighted to meet the nice looking guy. He was clean cut and handsome, wearing an air of self-confidence, which I especially liked. Our conversation during dinner was not only pleasant, but revealed that he was highly intelligent and well educated. Just as I was sizing him up to be marriage material, he began to tell me what he was looking for in a woman. I was caught by surprise and never saw this one coming.

He says, "I'm looking for a girl who is into fetishes."

I ask him what he means by that and he says, "Kinky things."

Intrigued by his straight forward approach, I couldn't help but ask him, "Like what?"

He says, "I like clothes pins clasped on my nipples and privates. I hope I'm not scaring you off."

Not one to be left hanging on a cliff, I act out the posture of a femme fatale and pretend to be innocent by answering, "Interesting."

With that, he says, "Then maybe I should tell you what really brings me to ecstasy. I like the pins taken off and replaced with needles."

I think I will stay focused on my career for a few more years.

Coming Into The Closet

Paul and I met on the internet and after two weeks, got together for our first date. He was a nice guy and clean cut by my standards. At the end of the evening, he paid for our dinner and walked me to my car, giving me a pleasant hug before inviting me to the movies on the following Friday. I agreed and we went our separate ways. It was that second date, movie night, when I got to know this "nice" guy much better.

Friday came and I met him in the parking lot of the theatre as we had agreed. When I arrived he was already there, greeting me with a warm smile and hug before heading into the show. We shared a large box of popcorn and half way through the movie held hands. It was all quite nice, I thought, so afterwards I invited him to follow me home for coffee and fresh pie.

Once we got to my apartment, he asked if he could use the bathroom and I pointed him in the direction through my bedroom. I turned on the television in the front room, and then went to the kitchen to make coffee, setting out plates to serve the homemade apple pie I had just baked earlier that afternoon. I decided to go with my expensive imported coffee and its wonderful aroma filled the air as the brew was finishing. I rearranged the table setting a second time, but Paul had still not returned from the bathroom. I was beginning to feel uncomfortable that it was taking him longer than normal.

I waited another few minutes before tiptoeing to my bedroom door to find out what happened to Paul. When I quietly peeked in, the bathroom door was open. He was nowhere to be seen. Then I noticed my closet light was on. There he was all right, with his pants down around his ankles as he was pleasuring himself with my panties. You heard right. My dresser drawer was open, and I guess he picked out several pairs of my panties. He was rubbing his "junk" on my intimate items. I freaked out and screamed, which obviously startled him, causing him to wheel around like an innocent kid caught in some naughty act. He began stuttering, saying over and over, "It's not what you think. It's not what you think."

"Get the hell out of my apartment before I call the police!" I howled.

He quickly pulled up his pants, dropped the panties to the floor and ran out of my apartment, slamming the door behind. I think I was in shock!

I was going to report Paul to the online site, but decided that although he had a serious problem, and a serious perversion, I didn't think it was my place to turn him in. I mean, he was harmless, but I was still struggling with whether I had a duty to other unsuspecting women to report him. Instead, I did the next best thing; I took myself offline. I think I'll just stick to the traditional ways of dating from now on. And you can bet that not only will it be a long time before I ever invite another man back to my apartment, but I will never make another pie.

Deal Killers

I've been a regular on two online dating sites for about three years now. During that time I've dated many different men and met a lot of real nice guys. I've also met a lot of guys with some serious baggage. I've learned to decline second or third dates from the latter list. Those on my "loser list" just don't work for me!

There are four men in particular who stand out in my memory and are ranked one through four on my loser list. These are guys I would NEVER see again because of their obvious issues, and I have names for all of them. They are Praying Pete, Racist Ryan, CoupOn Stephen (sorry, no cute rhyming in his name) and Really Robert.

Okay, so first is Praying Pete. Understand, I have no problem if someone wishes to pray before they go to bed or even over their food before they eat, but please don't take this gal to the movies and ask me to pray before the feature film starts. With all fairness to Pete, I did ask him about his beliefs for all the praying and he answered the question that night before we departed company. But honestly, his answer was so long I guess I missed the point or maybe I just didn't understand. He lost me after the first thirty minutes of his sermon and I found myself inspired to politely bid him, "Good night." Pete never got a second chance.

Next is Racist Ryan. I went out with him the year prior to the last Presidential election when Obama won his second term. Ryan's soapbox ranting was to blame the problems of the world and our struggling economy on Obama. He said we should never have voted that black man into office the first time. He said he realized things needed to change and people thought Obama would take us out of the mess that Bush left us in but, "Fool me once and elect that black guy into office again? We deserve the mess we're in today!" Sorry, Ryan, your passion for politics was way too bigoted for my appetite. I lost his phone number the minute I left the restaurant.

Then there was CoupOn Stephen. I wish his name had been Charlie so I could have tagged him CoupOn Charlie instead. That really would have sounded cuter. I should have known from the beginning when he named several choices of restaurants for our first date that he was one of those *twofer* one coupon people. The restaurants were all venues I'd never heard of or that I knew to be bad places to eat. By bad I mean crummy food or no ambiance or questionable location. But the light finally came on in my head when he in fact pulled out his *twofer* coupon at the end of our meal and actually asked the waitress if it was redeemable on a second visit to the place. No big deal because I was out of there at that point anyhow! The way I see it with that guy is even if they honored a reusable two-for-one dinner coupon for him, they wouldn't lose any money on the deal because he'll only be needing a table for one the rest of his life.

I've saved the fourth man on my loser list till last because I found him the most troubling. He is Really Robert, and his story is most troubling to me because he was the best looking of the bunch. As much as I would have liked to continue seeing him, his bit of baggage was a deal killer. It had to do with his living arrangement. It seems that Robert, who had been married until recently, was still living with his ex-wife in a two bedroom apartment. Okay, maybe finances could justify the necessity of their cohabitation, one housing expense instead of two, but when he told me that his twin sons lived there as well AND that he still slept in the same bed with his ex-wife, I knew my relationship with him had no future. My hat is off to him for being honest with me about it all. After all, he could have said he slept on the couch every night, right? He could have made no disclosure whatsoever about his living arrangement, right? He could have fabricated any sort of lie had he wished, but he didn't and that made my decision to put him on the loser list harder. As much as I detest a liar, this is the one time I would have accepted a little fib! But sorry Robert, your complete honesty killed the deal for me. Thanks anyway.

Now as for me, I have to say I am considered attractive. I'm college educated and can definitely hold my own in a conversation. I'm not boring nor do I preach my beliefs to others because I'm not even religious in a structured sense. I have good manners and am quite sexually oriented. All these traits seem to be appealing to most guys. I try not to be picky and never make impulsive or superficial judgments. While the dating pool seems to be getting smaller and smaller as the years go by, I'm trying to keep an open mind. I no longer imagine that I will find the perfect person, but there are a few hardline boundaries that I refuse to give up. As for my four losers, I must say I'd rather stay single the rest of my life than have to spend any more time with them. Sorry if they think I'm a bitch!

Take-Away: Everyone has some baggage. The question is whether or not you can live with someone else's or whether this excess baggage is a deal killer.

We'll Take
The Double-D's Please

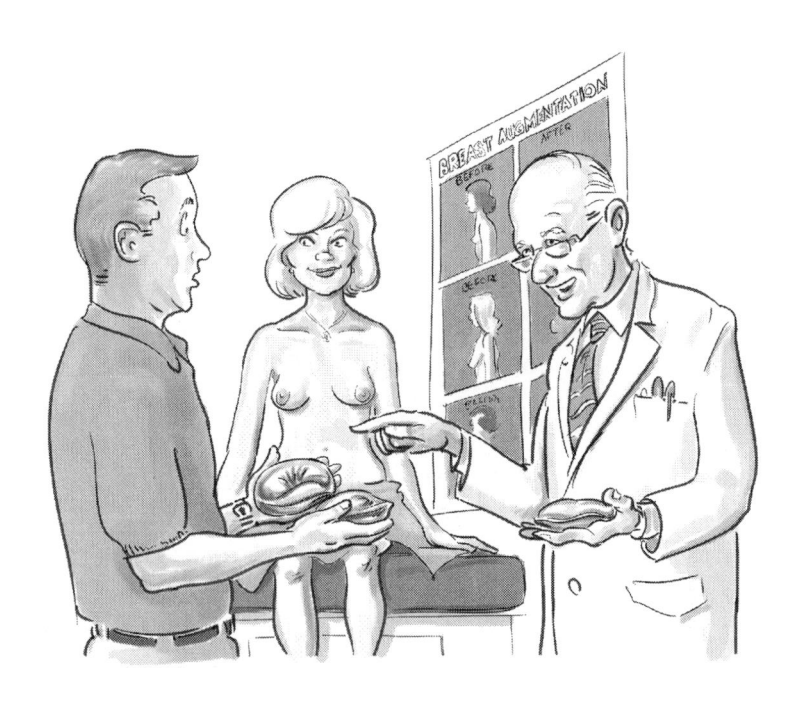

I met a girl online, chatted on the phone, exchanged pictures and really hit if off from the beginning. We made plans to meet at Ruth's Chris Steakhouse the following Saturday night and had a great time. We laughed a lot and discovered we had many things in common, which had me imagining I had finally met someone I could really fall for. We met up the next day, Sunday, for brunch and again enjoyed more laughs together. She told me about her family, where she grew up and was comfortable conversing on an even more personal level than the day before. I liked everything I heard. After we said goodbye that morning, I found myself anxious about getting to see her again soon.

The next day she called to invite me to meet for lunch. I promptly accepted. She then went on to explain that she had a doctor's consultation and that if I picked her up from the physician's office we could eat nearby. That plan was just fine by me so she gave me the address and assured me she would be finished with her appointment by 1 p.m.

When I arrived at the address I realized it was a cosmetic surgery facility. I wasn't really sure whether to go in or just park and wait, but I figured what the heck. So I walked into the reception area and took a seat. The receptionist asked me if she could help me and I told her I was waiting for a friend. She asked my friend's name and I replied, "Heidi." That's when I realized I didn't know her last name. I'm not sure if most people would think me a moron for that or give me a free pass for being thoughtlessly inept under the circumstances of it being a new friendship, but that old mean-looking receptionist gave me a very disapproving look. *Just HOW good of friends are you if you don't even know her last name?* Yeah, that thought was written all over the drill sergeant's face. I felt a flush of embarrassment as I returned to my seat and quickly pulled an open magazine up to the level of my nose then hunkered down low.

At any rate, I could still see her head behind the counter and heard her on the office phone system trying to locate Heidi. The next thing I know she announces that Heidi has requested that I join her in the examination room. I am now thinking to myself, *I hardly know this girl. Why does she want me to see her getting examined?* The commando receptionist opened the locked entrance door next to her station and pointed me down the hallway to Room D.

I was careful to make a quiet little tap on the door and when it opened, there sat Heidi topless with the doctor cupping her breasts.

I am certain Heidi saw the shock on my face, but commenced explaining that she wanted my opinion on what size to make her breasts. The doctor went right into expounding in detail on his augmentation procedure, handing me sample implants of varying sizes to squeeze and roll around for my approval. He explained the difference between saline and silicone. All of what he was saying was a blur in my ears, but I kept nodding my head for Heidi's sake as if I was genuinely engaged in understanding the information he was rattling off.

The whole scene was surreal to me. After all, I had just met this girl and here I am helping her pick out new breasts. I hadn't even had a glimpse of her old ones before ten minutes ago. Then the doctor asks Heidi which ones she feels most comfortable with and she answered, "It's up to Rob. He's the one who's going to be playing with them."

I think I must have uttered some unintelligible word and Heidi said, "Great." I handed the sample implants back to the doctor.

Once Heidi was dressed, I escorted her to the business office where we were greeted by a very warm and cheerful administrative assistant. She seats us at a round table and begins looking through some paperwork in front of her. First she wants to know when Heidi is available for the surgery and Heidi commits to a date. Next the lady asks ME how I would like to pay for the surgery and tells me they take all credit cards except American Express. My facial reaction to her question must have been priceless. I blurted out, "Do you take checks?" Okay, people, think about this: I am being asked to pay $6000 for a girl's boob job, a girl I just met two days earlier. I have no idea why I even asked the check question because I had no intention whatsoever of paying for this stranger's surgery. The assistant then said they couldn't take a personal check either and, thank you heaven above, she offered for me to think about the form of payment until next day since the surgery was two weeks off. I wanted to run out the door.

When Heidi and I left the office, I told her I was now running late for an appointment and couldn't make lunch. She asked if everything was okay and I lied, of course, before dashing away in my car.

I phoned her the next evening and told her what I was feeling. No, that's a lie. I didn't tell her everything I WANTED to say, but put it in terms of my investment being perhaps premature given the newness of our relationship. I suggested that we continue dating a little longer to make sure we were compatible as a couple before we increased her breast size. She sounded completely sincere in her response to me, She said she totally understood and was sorry I wasn't feeling the same romantic connection as her. She even added that she had no problem taking our relationship slower and promised to call me the next day.

I never heard from Heidi again.

Take-Away: Don't be a dumb boob to let girls take advantage of you, and don't ever meet your date at a cosmetic surgeon's office. Additionally, don't leave home without your American Express card. Many merchants don't take them...especially plastic surgeons.

Two Hours Equals Two Years

I met a gal on *Match.com*. Her name was Janice and what a great profile she had. It seemed that we both wanted similar things in a relationship and I had no qualms about her appearance based on the photos she had posted. We exchanged texts many times and although we hadn't yet talked on the phone, we made a date to meet at a local restaurant one evening after work. I was really looking forward to meeting her.

When I arrived at the restaurant, I recognized Janice right away. The first thing I noticed was that she actually looked like her profile photos. This was a huge relief since some of my past dates didn't always end up looking like their pictures. But to my delight, Janice's blue eyes and creamy complexion were even prettier in real life. However, the second thing I noticed was her voice. It was a nasally, whiny sounding voice and sounded vaguely familiar. I couldn't place it though.

We were seated right away and my first question was, "Have you met any interesting people on this dating site?"

What a mistake that was.

My conversation opener opened the floodgates! She went on and on and on about this date and then the next. She was on a rambling roll giving me her two year long, blow-by-blow dating history. I learned that a guy named James was a sex pervert and kept staring at her breasts all the time. Another guy, Milton, must have been 85 years old, but said he was 58. "If he was 58, I'm 24," Janice laughed. Someone else she went out with once was totally bald and looked like Kojack. Another guy was so skinny she thought he looked like a concentration camp survivor and Fred, oh my, her Fred dressed like he hadn't bought new clothes since the 1960's. After a while, I forgot what my original question to her was, but thank goodness the waitress came by and Janice had to take a breath to order her dinner.

I knew I was in for a bad evening.

Finally our dinner arrived and you would think putting food in her mouth would have given her, and me, a reprieve from the incessant chattering. No way. And even worse than her non-stop nasally voice was her laugh. It was so annoying I wanted to jump out of my skin every time she snorted it out.

The one good quality about her, other than her attractive looks, was that I really respected what she did for a living. She worked for hospice. I am very familiar with the work hospice does and knew it took a special kind of person to commit to caring for people who are seriously ill and in most cases terminal. I couldn't help but think how sorry I felt, though, for dying patients who had to listen to her banter all day and the sound of her annoying voice. The poor people had to have been thinking, "Please, please let me die in peace." I kept thinking, *Please, please let me dine in peace.*

Then it dawned on me whose voice hers reminded me of. On the television show "Friends", before the character Chandler married Monica, he dated a girl quite coincidentally also named Janice. She likewise had an annoying voice and laugh. Yes, my Janice was THAT person in the flesh…and ruining my dinner. At least had I been watching "Friends" on television I could have flipped the racket off, but here over dinner not so easy. I struggled to tune her out when I couldn't bare it any longer.

Two hours later I was paying the check. I realized that Janice was able to make our two hour dinner seem like an eternity. Then it dawned on me. If my last days were spent under hospice care, I would actually WANT Janice to care for me. She would make my last two hours on earth seem like two years. I couldn't wait to get her home

Please, please let me drive in peace.

My Date With A Bank Robber

I've dated all sorts of women over the years that I became acquainted with through online dating sites. There have been fat girls, skinny girls, women young and old, women from all walks of life and from all professions. You would think I've seen and heard it all by now and so did I until a few weeks ago.

I met a thirty-four year old woman on one of the more common sites. From her profile it looked as though she and I had plenty of similar interests. She loved fine dining, loved to laugh and loved the beach. But what really attracted me to her, aside from her cute pictures, was that she claimed to be a spontaneous person who loved to travel. That was the hook for me. I'd been searching for a woman who could pick up and take off on a moment's notice. I seriously want to take a lady to the most beautiful, scenic and romantic places in the world. I was hopeful that Amy would be the one.

So we met at a sports pub and grill and had the greatest time talking and watching the NCAA March Madness on the TV monitors and big screen. I asked Amy a question that I have asked a lot of my dates, and her answer came as quite a surprise.

The question was: Will you tell me something about yourself that wouldn't be on a profile and only something I'd find out if we dated for a long time?

She smiled as if she quickly had an answer and replied, "I have something you probably don't hear from most of your dates. Ready? I was arrested for robbing a bank."

I thought I misunderstood her. "Excuse me?"

The story she told was that her ex-boyfriend was the actual bank robber, committing the heist together with a friend of his. Amy was considered an accomplice to the crime because she drove the getaway car. She filled in a few more casual details to the story as if being a bank robber was a common occurrence that most anyone could relate to, but frankly I didn't know how to respond. I paused for a furtive moment and then asked, "Did you go to jail?"

Amy cracked a little smile and went on to explain that she didn't go to jail. She pled guilty to lesser charges and had to do community service work for her involvement.

"But, no jail time when you drove the getaway car? How is that possible?"

She explained that she served as a witness at the trial and told her story in court. She exposed those involved in the crime and because she identified her ex and his friend, she was given a lesser sentence. No jail time.

"Did you know ahead of time that you were actually going to be the getaway driver?"

She shook her head affirming that to be a fact, but went on to explain that she didn't really know who they were going to rob. She thought they were going to rough someone up over an unpaid gambling debt. She thought it was a sort of justified revenge on somebody who owed them money and they were acting as debt collectors on their own behalf. She didn't ask any intrusive questions; she just did what they told her to do. It was simple as that.

Maybe it was simple in her mind, but not to me. It was a date I won't forget anytime soon. I haven't seen Amy again since that evening. I don't know whether it's because I'm busy at work or because it wasn't really ever my vision to have a criminal for a wife one day. Whatever the reason, I admit she was a great girl, beautiful and honest. I promised the secret of her past would remain safe with me.

Take-Away: Do not ask your first date to tell you something that they normally would never tell someone until after they've known them for a long time. It sounds like a fun game to play, but trust me, most of the time, this disclosure will be a deal killer. There is plenty of time to get to know one another before something serious is disclosed.

Dating Myself

Recently I had a date with a girl who I met on a dating site called *What's Your Price*. It's a site where older guys like me seek younger women to accompany them to dinner, a movie or any occasion that a date is an appropriate companion. Now that I am over fifty, I like the idea of having a young, pretty woman on my arm, or so I thought.

I arranged my first date from the site after combing through numerous profiles. The beautiful young lady I chose was named Brittany, and for the sake of keeping a positive attitude, we shall assume that was in fact her real name. I thought she would be great company over dinner while I was travelling through a city west of the Mississippi and whether her stats were true or false, I really didn't care since I had no marriage intentions with a woman thirty years my junior.

I greeted Brittany in the front courtyard of the restaurant where we had agreed to meet. She looked like a Barbie doll wearing a very sexy, low cut black mini dress. She made me feel a little frisky as she took my arm and we strolled into the dining room. Every guy in the place took a double take as we passed by.

They were probably imagining me to be the lucky dog that was going to have sex with this gorgeous young blond, but that wasn't my intent. Brittany was only twenty years old.

Once we were seated, I tried to start conversation with Brittany. It wasn't so easy to do. I found out pretty quickly that we didn't really have much in common. Then, I thought of a brilliant idea. Rather than continuing to strain for conversation with this young lady, I would make the table talk a game. It was an idea I learned from my niece, who was actually two years younger than Brittany.

I asked my date if she had ever heard or seen any of the following: a typewriter, a rotary telephone, yellow pages, a VHS videotape, a cassette player, a gas station where attendants pumped your gas, Pac-Man, the Carol Burnet Show or Johnny Carson. Brittany looked at me like I was talking a foreign language. She said she had seen a typewriter once, but never used one. She also had seen yellow pages, but had never seen a standing telephone booth.

Then I asked her if she knew what a Polaroid camera was. She said she'd heard of them but hadn't ever seen one, must less used one. She wanted to know what was so special about them, so I had to explain they were the first cameras that gave you the picture right then and there. She then ever-so-smartly informed me that they have those now in camera phones. OK. I pursued this little conversation game for a while longer but all I was accomplishing was to date myself even more pathetically. She really made me feel stone-aged when I told her about my record player back in college and all my albums. And then she became completely perplexed when I told her that there were no ATM machines for instant cash back then. She asked, "Well, where did your money come from?" Yes, I'm stone-aged and she had probably never even heard of the Stone Age!

We made it through dinner and hugged and said our goodbyes. I think we both knew that we wouldn't be seeing each other again, and I realized that I needed to take this site off my favorites because I didn't want to continue to play games whenever I wanted company at dinner.

Take-Away: Guys, younger girls are not necessarily the answer. When their looks are gone, you are definitely going to need substance, and when you really think about it, what do they really see in you besides the obvious security blanket. Don't rule out more mature women. They tend to be more sophisticated, more experienced, and more willing to ignore some of your bad habits and excess baggage. Just a suggestion.

Five Drink Rule

Here's a story that I can laugh about now, but it wasn't too funny at the time it happened.

I met a nice girl on a site called *Seeking Arrangement's*. We decided to meet for dinner one evening, and I picked a popular Italian restaurant in her town where we were to meet at 7:00 p.m. I thought making the drive convenient for her was the gentlemanly thing to do.

She arrived before I did. I greeted her in the bar where she had already ordered herself a glass of wine. I paid the bar tab and we were then escorted to our table. We were seated outdoors in a beautiful courtyard setting. There were specialty shops all around, and lots of people leisurely milling about. Cheryl ordered another glass of wine and I settled back in my chair with a bottle of beer. It was a relaxing atmosphere under a full summer moon.

After examining the menu, we ordered an eggplant dish and beef Carpaccio as appetizers. Cheryl started right in with stories about her dating adventures and work fiascos. She ordered another glass of wine. Her animated stories were entertaining, but when the waiter arrived to take our dinner order and she ordered a fourth glass of wine, I began to wonder about her drinking so much. Normally I wouldn't give a thought to how much someone was drinking, and although her wine was pricey at $15 a glass I was really more concerned about her well-being and condition than the amount of my bill. I thought her drinking seemed excessive given that we hadn't even started dinner yet.

Our meal arrived and we both thoroughly enjoyed the food. Cheryl went for her fifth glass of wine. We continued sharing some lively old war stories and when we had finished our meal, the waitress asked whether we wanted dessert. We decided to share some tiramisu with cappuccinos. Then, just as the waitress was walking away Cheryl flagged her back and requested a Bailey's Irish Cream on the side, straight up. Cheryl was slurring her words pretty badly at this point and I was beginning to wonder whether she was going to be fit to safely drive herself home. She wasn't.

So when we were heading to the parking lot to leave, I offered to drive my date home. She didn't argue at all nor did she show the least concern about her car being left behind .She was definitely in no condition to be driving, and once she was buckled up in my car, she said she wasn't feeling too well. "It must have been something I ate," she mumbled. "Yea," I consoled, "Italian food can be a little rich sometimes."

So out of the lot we went and it took five minutes to get Cheryl to tell me whether to turn left or right because I had no idea how to get to her house. Down the road we went and she had me do a U- turn because she forgot to tell me to make a right at the last intersection. We weren't doing very well and to make matters worse, she then gave me a look that said there was a problem. She was pale. Just as I was going to ask if she wanted me to pull over, it was too late. She dropped her head between her knees and threw up. Yes, all over my nice new car. I thought I was going to get sick then because of the smell, but I hung tuff and pulled the car off the roadway and onto a grassy area. She leaned out the passenger door and threw up again. I'm sorry, but just hearing someone getting sick is enough to make me feel queasy, but I hung tuff a second time. I helped her wipe her face with a tissue and relax.

We finally got to Cheryl's condo where I stood her up and helped her into her place. I even had to dig through her purse to find her door keys, if that tells you how out of it she was. After pulling off her shoes and laying her down on her couch, I could tell she was sobering up a bit. She assured me she was fine and then started apologizing profusely. Poor drunk Cheryl. She really was a mess.

I couldn't wait to get the heck out of there and knew that would be the last I saw her. I texted her the following day to make sure she was okay. She texted back apologizing again and saying she felt awful that she had gotten sick in my car. I told her not to worry and that I'd speak to her soon.

Never called Cheryl again!

What Kind of Car Do You Drive?

First, I want to say that I've been cruising online dating sites for several years. I will admit that I would love to find a guy who is rich, successful and good looking, but I've decided my chances of that happening are about the same as hitting the Powerball. Nonetheless, I still zero in on the profiles that show a good stated income and I'll give them a wink just for the money, but that's not the sole basis for my winking at a man online. There are other important details to consider and until recently, I'd never thought about finding out what kind of car a guy drives before accepting a first date. Do you think it would be too tacky to ask up front?

I met Steven online. He seemed like a really nice guy and after several conversations we decided to go out together. Our first date was at a Carrabba's Grill, which is a chain of Italian restaurants. The plan was to meet in the lobby of the restaurant at 7:00 p.m. Steven was already there when I arrived. He was polite, funny and quite the entertainer the whole evening as we got to know each other better. We both enjoyed outdoor sports and were dog-lovers, both of us by coincidence owning chocolate Labradors. He worked for an exterminating company and told me several hair-raising stories of encounters he'd had with insects while performing his job. It was obvious he really liked both his work and his boss, but said, "Of course there are certain things that bug me." I got the joke right away.

After this successful first date, I decided I wanted to get to know Steven better so I accepted his invitation to go out the following weekend. We agreed that he would pick me up at my condo Saturday evening at 6:00 p.m. I was pretty excited about seeing him again and since it was middle of summer, I dressed in a sexy little short dress with heels and a large bag that matched. I thought I looked quite spiffy with my tanned legs and hot-pink ensemble. Steven arrived on the mark and waltzed me out of the lobby to the parking lot where he had parked in the visitor's section. We strolled around the corner of the building and I was suddenly mortified at the sight of what I knew had to be my limo ride for the evening. I was horrified to see a bright yellow Volkswagen Bug. This was not just a regular yellow VW bug as you might imagine, this was a BUG. The vehicle actually looked like a giant bug with antenna and hairy legs sticking out the side. There was a tail too and now that I reflect on it, maybe it was a mouse instead of a bug because there were big black things on top that may have been its ears. Either way, I was mortified by the embarrassment of being seen in that thing. I tried to hide my shock.

Gentleman Steven opened the door for me with a big old smile on his face, explaining that driving the company car was one of the perks of his job. He was quite proud to be sporting his date around in the "whatever" car. I wanted to slide down in my seat so no one would see me.

We had a nice dinner, but honestly, my heart just wasn't in it. I couldn't date a man who saw nothing wrong with driving a bug or mouse around town. I tried to pretend that nothing was wrong, but I guess I'm not a very good actress. Steven noticed that I had been quiet and after driving me home asked if I was okay. I said of course, which was a lie. He then gave me a little peck on the cheek. I could tell he was stalling in the hopes of an after dinner invitation up to my condo, but that wasn't going to happen. No way! I thanked him for dinner and said I'd talk to him during the week, another lie. We never spoke again.

In a way I feel sort of bad because Steven was a really nice guy and, you know, things could have been worse. What if he had been a hotdog salesman driving the Oscar Meyer Weiner- Mobile.

Take-Away: Be wary of those who ask you upfront what kind of car do you drive. It's usually a red flag and a way of them finding out whether you're successful or not. It's usually not to find out whether you work for an exterminating or a hot dog company

Bats All Folks!

I've been dating women lately on an online travel dating site. One holiday weekend I decided to fly to Austin, Texas to meet Brenda. She presented herself to be a sexy gal with spunk which interested me, and since I'd never been to Austin thought my trip would have a double purpose. So I booked my five hour flight for that Memorial Day weekend with high expectations of spending the time with an appealing lady and touring the happening town.

When Brenda greeted me at the airport baggage claim I knew right away this was not going to be a successful vacation. First of all, she looked nothing like her online photos. I'd say they must have been taken at least ten years earlier. Secondly, she was dressed in a biker outfit, which couldn't have been more of a mismatch to my usual preppy style. And did I mention tattoos? I sure don't remember seeing any tattoos in those online photos. I must have been either blind as a bat (which I'm not) or she had them covered up. Who knows? Maybe they were brand new? Whatever the case, it didn't matter because I found them to be a turn off. I wanted to gather up my bags, cut the losses and go back home right then. I could see nothing positive happening between the two of us, but there I was with no polite way out at this point.

When I stepped outside the airport it must have been 120 degrees. By the time we reached Brenda's car in the parking lot my shirt was totally wet from perspiration, and I forced myself to appear like an enthusiastic date, but she got my vibe. During our drive to the Hyatt where I was booked, we made small talk and I forced myself to appear more upbeat to avoid hurting her feelings. She dropped me off and said she'd be back in a few hours to walk to the downtown district for dinner. I hoped that would be a positive experience since Austin is known to be a party city.

Brenda picked me up as planned and I noticed she had dressed up. At least now our mismatched appearance together didn't stand out like a sore thumb, but she still didn't resemble the hot sexy girl I remembered from her profile pictures. We strolled over the main bridge in town to our restaurant and had a nice dinner. The steakhouse was above average and we relaxed with a few drinks before venturing out again. Brenda had told me earlier that Austin was really known for its music and bars, but failed to mention it was pretty dead when all the college students left town for the summer. Most students were gone at this point.

After dinner we strolled back toward the bridge and I noticed a crowd of people gathered there. I asked Brenda what was going on and she explained that every night hundreds of people come to watch the bats fly out.

"Excuse me?"

"Yes," she said. "This is Austin's famous Congress Bridge. Every night more than a million and a half bats fly out and the event has captured the attention of visitors and residents from all over." "If you're not kidding, Brenda," I said, " then hold on just one little minute and let me enlighten you. Back home where I come from if we saw one disgusting bat we would be running!"

From my perspective, being in a place swarmed by over a million bats might be a great idea for the television show "Fear Factor", but it's not my cup of tea under any circumstance. If that was supposed to be one of Austin's major attractions, then get me out of there. That's all folks! I left for home the next morning. I'd seen enough and flew home like a bat out of hell with no intentions of ever going back or speaking to Brenda again.

***Take-Away:** Although Austin is a "hot" place to visit, not so much in the summer…..although it was 120 degrees!*

My $1200 Dinner Date

First, I want to make it clear that I had no intention of having dinner with an escort. It was just supposed to be a simple dinner date with a girl I met on *Match*. I think I got snookered.

I had a successful real estate closing that week so I decided to splurge a little and take my date to a higher priced steakhouse in Boca Raton, Florida. We arranged to meet at 8 p.m. and as it happened, arrived at the front door of the place at exactly the same time. I recognized her immediately from the pictures in her site; she had a noticeably pretty face. What I didn't recognize though was the rest of her body.

As we meandered over to the bar, it seemed every guy in the restaurant was staring at my date. Frankly, I was feeling a little embarrassed because her appearance was such an obvious attention-getter. She was wearing a shiny silver mini skirt that barely covered her tush and a revealing blouse with stretchy material pulled to its limits over her double-D breasts. At her waist was a jet-blue belt studded with rhinestones that hung heavily over her hipline, and did I mention the over-the-knee boots?

Parking ourselves at the bar, I asked my date what she would like to drink. She requested champagne, and for myself ordered my usual Grey Goose on the rocks. During our wait to be seated for dinner, we carried on small talk, and then she ordered another glass of champagne. I was yet only half finished with my original cocktail, but thankfully the hostess was prompt to seat us and I paid the bar tab of $75.00. I double checked the itemized ticket to be sure it was not in error since it seemed a bit pricey for three drinks. I walked to our dinner table feeling slightly victimized by financial extortion.

Once seated, my date ordered another glass of champagne, then as an afterthought suggested a bottle instead to last during our meal. The waiter then described their dinner specials for the evening and recommended the fresh lobster, flown in that day and weighing in between three and four pounds each. I somehow didn't hear the price per pound, but it was clear my date had no concerns about cost. She was in the mood for lobster and that was just the way it was going to be! She was apparently in the mood for stone crab too and promptly ordered the appetizer platter.

I have no idea why I was going along with what seemed like an ambush on my pocketbook, but I did. Maybe that big commission check I earned earlier in the week had affected my otherwise reasonable ego, making me imagine myself to be Daddy Bigbucks. Perhaps I had become hypnotized by her huge breasts staring at me across the table. Whatever the reason, I estimated I was out at least $500 thus far and I hadn't even ordered my meal yet. This fine dining tab then grew even larger with a second bottle of champagne, amazing after dinner soufflés and tip. All told, I was out nearly $1200, and I began to surmise that I was going to need a big sale every week to keep THIS woman in the style she was obviously accustomed to.

When we were leaving the restaurant, she asked me if I lived anywhere close by. It seemed she was hinting that she'd like to pay me back for the dinner in her "special way" however, since I lived more than half hour away, her overture didn't really matter to me. Getting hit so hard in the wallet killed any possible love connection I might otherwise have had. Actually, I felt totally taken advantage of so I tried to wrap things up by saying I had enjoyed the evening with her and thought we could get together again in the future. She gave me a very sweet kiss on the cheek and thanked me for dinner. She said she would be looking forward to seeing me again and even asked if I was free the following night. I think I got locked in a momentary shock-stare of disbelief when I heard that, but luckily the valet pulled up with my car just in time to give me an escape. I watched in my rearview mirror as she got into her Hummer behind me. I then regained some sense of power once I gripped the steering wheel of my car. Was she a professional dater or what?

Take Away: *Watch out for women who order the most expensive things on a menu. Their intentions may not always be good. Consider limiting first dates to either drinks or coffee meetings.*

All She Could Eat

Michelle is a girl I met online. After several phone conversations, I decided to invite her for a dinner date. I learned that she loved lobster and liked to gamble so I made a plan for our get together that included both. Since she lived in Connecticut as did I, and it just so happened I knew of a place not too far away known for having the best seafood buffet in the state. It was also probably one of the only places in the country that offers all you can eat Maine lobsters. The casino was located close by.

I picked her up that evening and drove to a restaurant called Custy's. As it turned out, she hadn't exaggerated earlier comments about lobster - Michelle REALLY loved lobster. She must have had six of them while we talked and laughed for a couple of hours over dinner.

During the course of our meal, I found her to be a very down to earth person. She was pretty and had an overall look that appealed to me, but most noticeable was that she didn't put on airs like most women I've dated. I can't imagine any of them from my past who would have ordered even two lobsters for fear of looking like a pig. It takes a special girl with no false pretenses to eat six in front of a guy she hardly knows. I thought that was actually pretty courageous on her part to have no fear in being herself.

It was getting close to ten o'clock and I was ready for coffee and dessert. Michelle declined to have either. She said she was starting to feel a bit queasy and thought maybe she had overeaten. Frankly, I thought she had overeaten when she ordered lobster number three. I could see from the color in her face she was uncomfortable, but she was a trooper about it and held her chin up for more conversation while I finished my dessert. Hoping to surprise her and get her mind off the upset stomach, I told her of my plan to go to the casino next. She perked up a bit and seemed excited about my thoughtfulness to take her, but as we were heading out of the restaurant she whispered in my ear that maybe she would have to pass on the casino idea. She asked if we could do it another time as she was feeling a little worse.

As I was driving her home, she looked quite out of it. I asked if she was okay, but she confessed she was really feeling terrible.

"Is there anything I can do?"

That's when she asked me to find a rest area on the highway where I could pull over.

Poor girl. Next thing I knew, she bent over with her head between her knees and began heaving. How I ever managed getting off the side of the road without incident I'll never know, because the heaving became projectile-like, distracting me terribly from watching where I was driving. But I did get safely over and parked. I began patting her back hoping it would somehow help.

All over the floor of my car was her regurgitated dinner.

By the time I got Michelle home, the good news was that she was feeling better. She couldn't stop apologizing. The other good news was that she insisted on taking the floor mat out herself and pitching it in the garbage can next to her driveway. I can't over emphasize how much I appreciated that, otherwise I'm not sure I would have made it back to my place without an abdominal medical emergency of my own.

I later learned that she had had an allergic reaction, similar to a poisoning, from the iodine in the all those lobsters she had eaten. It totally overdosed her. When that happens to a person, the best thing they can do is to throw it up. Well, had you seen the floor of my car you'd know she accomplished that mission very well. (But why in my car?)

This was probably the most memorable first date I've ever had, and even though we went out a couple of times after that, we never did make it to the casino.

Pizza Disaster

I met a girl online and after speaking with her many times by phone, we decided to meet one Sunday night at a very popular, local pizza restaurant. She said it was her favorite. On my own, I would have never gone there because of the long waiting lines outside the little place that only had capacity to seat maybe fifty people at a time. But their pizzas were so well liked, most people didn't mind having to wait a couple of hours to get the famous coal oven pizza.

When I told my date I didn't want to wait so long for pizza, she said not to worry and was proud to say she knew the owners of the place very well. She could call ahead of time and we wouldn't have to wait. With that accommodation, I agreed to meet her there. It was a date.

When I arrived I recognized her right away from her profile picture. As was no surprise, there was a long line of people, but Christina led me around the side of the building and we went in the back door. I surmised it was the owner's son who then took us to a table in the restaurant. So far, I was happy with the service.

It took about fifteen minutes before a waitress arrived at our table, took our drink order and gave us menus. It struck me as unusual to see a waitress who looked to be in her seventies, especially in such a crowded and busy place. Christina said she knew her to have been with the restaurant forever, and from my observation, it showed. Christina said her name was Fay.

Well, we didn't see Fay again for another twenty minutes, and finally she showed up at a table near us that had been seated after we arrived some thirty minutes earlier. I got Fay's attention and told her we were ready to order. She said she'd be right back.

Meanwhile, a young couple was just being seated adjacent to us. I remarked to Christina that they looked like they were on their first date too. She agreed.

Then I noticed Fay heading in our direction and since I was beginning to get really hungry, I forced a smile at her thinking she was coming for our order. She smiled back, holding up one finger as if to say she'd be a minute and then went to the table where the young couple had just been seated. Now keep in mind that we have been there for nearly forty-five minutes and still haven't ordered.

So, Fay finally steps over to our table and says, "Have you had time to look over the menu?" I wanted to say we've had time to read War and Peace, but I didn't want to risk the possibility of my sarcasm slowing things down even more, so I kept my mouth closed. Christina ordered the pizza we agreed on earlier, which was their most popular, a white clam pie, and Fay writes it down on her pad before heading off to the kitchen. I watch skeptically as she clips the ticket to the cook's lineup of orders and with little faith in this elderly woman's waitressing skill, hoped she put it in the right place. Fay then returns to take the order from the young couple adjacent to us. I overhead them ordering the white clam pie as we had.

This is where things begin to get interesting. About twenty-five minutes later, here comes Fay heading toward us with our white pizza. My mouth is watering, but what? She sets the pizza down at the table adjacent to us, you know, the young couple who came in twenty-five minutes after us and then ordered ten minutes after we placed our order. Yeah, that same couple. I couldn't take it anymore.

I said, "Fay, isn't that our pizza?" She replies, "What did you order?"

I'm exasperated. I'm thinking, *My waitress is asking me what I ordered as if she had no idea?* So I excuse myself and go to the counter at the kitchen window and say to the hostess, "I've been waiting for over an hour and our waitress just gave our order to someone else."

The hostess said, "I'm so sorry. Do you want to place another order?"
"Another order", I said? " No. I want my original order now!"

Fay comes by and hears me talking loudly to this woman, then says to her, "I'm sorry, I forgot to put their order in."

If you could have monitored my heart rate at that point, it surely would have broken the record of extreme odds against a person surviving a heart attack, much less being able to tell about it after the fact. Steam was coming from my ears. Enough with the nice talk, I thought, and went into commando mode, "You forgot to place my order? I've been here over an hour and you gave my pizza away to people who came in thirty minutes after me?"

Fay looked confused.

A pizza maker who heard me arguing at the counter leans over and says, "What's your problem, buddy?"

I go into a rant telling him that I believe my waitress has gone senile as I'm no closer to getting my pizza than I was an hour ago, then finishing my tirade with saying, "and she fricking forgot to place my order!"

"You're calling my mother senile?" And with that the gorilla jumps over the counter and throws me to the ground where we begin swinging wildly at each other and rolling around on the floor. The scuffle was out of control and from the corner of my eye I see Christina hovering above us with a terrified look on her face. For one hopeful moment I thought maybe she might have some clout to rescue me from the bruiser who was wailing on me, but she didn't.

The brawl was finally broken up by some other employees and customers, and I was manhandled out the door and told never to come back. This was probably my worst date experience ever. Not only didn't I get the girl, but never got my pizza either.

Take-Away: Guys, how many times do I have to tell you? Don't let your date pick the restaurant. There is seldom a good benefit coming out of this decision for you....even if it is only pizza.

Food Fight

I took a date to a cute little Italian restaurant in New Haven, Connecticut. The place only had about fifty seats in it with small, two-person tables covered with classic red checkered table cloths. In the middle of the deep, but narrow room is one long table where I took notice of a family group of maybe twelve people who were seated and seemed to be celebrating an anniversary. They were a noticeably rowdy bunch and thoroughly enjoying themselves, laughing and bantering back and forth.

As I steered my date toward our table close to the front door, I couldn't help but notice the heavy set gentleman at the head of the big table. He had a large belly and was unattractive, his face slightly scarred from acne and somewhat discolored. A fat cigar hung out of his mouth. The big guy reminded me of a character from The Sopranos television series. He really looked Mafia. Seated to his left side was a gorgeous buxom blonde wearing a revealingly low cut blouse.

At any rate, as this is a first date with someone I met online, I'm wanting to make a good impression so I bring her to this particular restaurant because I frequent the place and am familiar with the staff. As we enter the front door, the bartender hollers a greeting across the room to me by name and when the waitress comes to our table, she asks if I want my usual martini on the rocks. I can tell my date is impressed by this personalized service. It makes me look like somebody important.

We start out with drinks and appetizers and our conversation is going well. My new lady acquaintance is giving me every indication that the stage is set for us to have a nice evening. I'm feeling at home with her and see no need to put on my usual date-face so I kick back in my chair to relax.

Things continue going along between us for about half hour, until it happens that the waiter sets a tray of food on the empty table behind me and commences serving some dishes from it to a couple sitting adjacent to us. Just as the waiter puts down the first bowl, with what looks like steaming hot veal parmesan, the heavy set gentleman with the fat cigar stands up from the big table in the center of the room and barks out loud at the waiter, "Hey. Isn't that our food?" He defiantly ashes his cigar on the floor while throwing his other hand upward with a well-known Italian gesture.

"No, sir, yours should be coming out shortly."

"Shortly?" Mr. Soprano says and challenges the waiter by saying, "We sat down before those people. What is this?"

"Sir, they didn't order appetizers so I put their check in right away."

With that, Soprano turns red in the face and reaches for the tray with hot plates still on it and says, "they're not eating before me." He then flips the tray over, sending spaghetti and sauce against the wall. In the midst of breaking glassware and silverware ricocheting off the floor, several people sitting nearby scramble to hide under tables, no doubt expecting gunfire to erupt at any moment. Then the room goes silent. Globs of spaghetti slide down the wall and dangle from the back of a chair, dripping even more red stuff into the mess.

So much for my first romantic dinner with Stephanie. Across the table from me, she is literally white in the face and clasping her chest in fear, too terrified to move.

The whole table of Soprano people begin gathering up their belongings and get up to leave, slamming a few chairs around in the process. Tony steps into the aisle and heads for the front door with his insulted gang close behind in a mass exit. Soprano says, "Let's get the hell out of here." With that, he grabs a wine rack on the way, sending about a hundred bottles of wine crashing to the floor. The door closes behind them with a bang.

Everyone in the restaurant is petrified.

The chef immediately begins apologizing and pacing around, patting the patrons' shoulders to calm them down. He assures us that the police have been called, and begs everyone to stay and have drinks on the house. It takes a little while, but the tensions begin to ease up and most people stay for their meal. However, Stephanie is still so shaken that she wants me to take her home. I'm thinking about asking to take my food to go, but figure that would be an insensitive thing to do given my date's obvious level of anxiety. I honor her request. We leave before the police arrive.

It was an interesting evening to say the least. I never saw Stephanie again.

Texting While Dining

How do you feel when this happens?

Say you're out on a first date and you notice your new acquaintance has his or her head down while fiddling with their cell phone under the table. Or, maybe he or she isn't even hiding the fact that they're having a private text conversation with someone else while you sit there playing second fiddle to their phone. Either way, you'd probably surmise that your date finds texting more entertaining than you and most likely a sign that he or she just isn't that into you, right? That's how it seems to me. But ultimately I've decided to look on the brighter side and not take it personally. I chalk it up as a sign of the times.

Now don't misunderstand me, that doesn't mean I don't find it annoying. And now that I think about it, I can name a few other things I've found annoying in the past such as my date being late, drinking too much or ordering the most expensive thing on the menu. But none of those compare to a woman who texts all evening or one who is on the phone constantly, especially with her children. That drives me plumb loco! With the rise in text messaging over the years from one million texts a month to seventy-five billion, it's clear that people have been caught up in texting frenzy. The real problem though is that when it becomes a rude behavior, many texting fans don't seem to care.

Texting While Dining

My last girlfriend who I met online was beautiful, smart and loving. Her only flaw was that she would text all the time when we were together. It didn't matter if we were at a party, out to dinner, lounging around the pool or at a movie, she'd be texting 24/7. I told her it was something that bothered me. I told her I thought it was rude and inconsiderate. She'd stop temporarily, but her irritating habit would inevitably show back up within a short period of time. She was addicted. She just couldn't stop.

I finally had enough. I realized I was brooding every time I'd see her on the phone or texting someone. It started to make me crazy and undermine my otherwise healthy sense of security. I imagined she was texting other men or an ex-boyfriend. When I began wondering if she was text-talking behind my back, I knew it was time to take action before a full-blown attack of paranoia overtook me. I needed to end the relationship and decided to do it in a way that she could best relate: communication via text.

Me: Hey cutie, did you hear about that new movie that just came out called 'Other People'?

She: No, sweetie.

Me: Well, that's who I want to start seeing. I've had enough.

She: Go f… yourself and have a good life.

I never heard from her again, and I feel like my old self again!

Take-Away: *Don't text over dinner. It sends the message that you're not interested in your date. Even if you aren't, it's still rude and disrespectful.*

Family Ties

I met a great girl online several years ago. Her name was Terri. She was petite with short black hair that highlighted her small frame perfectly. Because she was a dancer, she was in great shape. I thought she was the cutest thing I'd ever seen. She came from a strong Italian family background and with my Jewish Russian heritage, we had many similar values. We got along great from the very beginning.

We had been dating for several weeks and Terri invited me to a Sunday family dinner. She explained that although they called it a dinner, the get-together actually started each Sunday at 1 p.m. It always included a large group of her relatives: aunts, uncles, sister, brother, nieces, nephews, in laws and her mother. None of them ever missed being there because they held it as an important family tradition. Although I thought it seemed a bit premature in our relationship to be invited to meet the whole family, I figured what the heck. I liked Terri a lot so I accepted the invitation.

The dinner was at Terri's mother's house and to make a good impression, I dressed in my Sunday best, a tie, jacket and dress slacks. When I arrived that day, I was greeted at the door by Terri's brother-in-law, Vinnie. I was more than shocked to see him standing there dressed in boxer shorts and an undershirt. Adding to that, his crew necked t-shirt was stretched so tight over his fat gut it made his belly button stand out like a sore thumb. Trust me, it was a real attention-getter, but I somehow managed to keep my eyes on his face instead of his belly as he welcomed me in.

Once inside, there were about a half dozen babies in the front room and living room, some crawling around the floor and some in baby-playpens. They were all barefooted infants and wearing nothing but diapers and little baby-type tops. Terri's sister introduced herself next and seemed to think nothing of the fact that she was still dressed in her pajamas. I surmised at that point the mother's house was home to more than just Terri's mother. It appeared to be one big laid back family living under the same roof. Then one by one, all the other family members filtered in from other rooms to greet me, and Terri led me to the kitchen to meet her mother. Everyone there was dressed so casually I began feeling ridiculous in my tie and jacket, but oh well I couldn't have shown up as a guest wearing nothing but my boxers could I?

Shortly after my arrival, the whole troop began gathering around the dinner table. It looked to me like mass chaos as chairs were situated and plates were being shuffled around to make room for everyone. There were rowdy conversations going on from opposite ends of the table and no one seemed to think a thing of talking over anyone else. It was completely hectic but for a brief moment of silence when Terri's brother-in-law said a prayer, then the chaos and clamor started up again. I guess you would say this was authentic family dining, Italian-style! I was starving hungry and, I have to admit, the food smelled delicious! Bowls of vegetables and baskets of bread flew around the table with everyone taking heaping portions. Terri's mother fetched a large pot of steaming sauce from the kitchen, which she began scooping over everyone's pasta. Terri flopped a large rolled up thing on my plate that looked like a giant sausage and when Vinnie saw me cut into it, he made a joke that it looked like a male organ. That brought a huge roar of laughter from the already boisterous group. Personally, I was a bit taken back by his comment and for a moment thought I was going to lose my appetite after listening to his phallic description of the thing. I kept my thoughts to myself though and tried my best to go with the flow. We all dug in heartily.

As the food fest went on, Terri explained to me what it was I was eating. She called it braciole, which is some kind of meat with stuffing wrapped up inside it. It was actually very tasty and I was thoroughly enjoying it until something got stuck in my throat. I started choking. At first, nobody realized I was having a problem. I couldn't get air in or out and felt myself starting to turn red in the face. Something was lodged down in my airway, but with all the commotion going on at the table no one noticed my guttural heaving. Desperation overtook me. I jumped to my feet and lurched forward, jamming my fingers down my throat in the hopes of saving my own life. I pulled out what felt like a piece of rope. I couldn't believe my eyes. The room fell silent and everyone was staring at me.

"What the hell is a piece of rope doing in my mouth?"

With the rope and that question blurted out of my mouth, everyone burst into laughter. As it turns out, braciole always has a twine attached to hold the meaty thing together while it is being cooked. The whole family thought it hysterical that I would think I should eat it, but the truth was I didn't even know it was there because it had been buried under the momma's scoops of sauce. It would have been nice had someone warned me ahead of time of the hidden hazard!

"You're supposed to remove the string before eating," they laughed and howled. Vinnie especially roared over my blunder and seized the opportunity to throw out even more phallic sausage jokes. Yes, that whole Italian family ribbed me mercilessly for trying to eat the delicious and savory string. Frankly, I failed to see the humor they found in watching their guest of honor, me, almost die as I was choking to death.

I didn't see Terri too many times after that. I was totally turned off by everything I had witnessed at her Sunday family dinner. I just couldn't envision that our families would ever fit in with each if our relationship progressed. In retrospect, I'm not sure if it was a mistake or a God-send to meet Terri's whole family so early on in our relationship…especially her brother-in-law Vinnie.

Take-Away: In the dating world, there will always be strings attached . Don't be so eager to meet the family right away. Get to know each other first before you bring friends and family into the equation.

Your Kitchen Is On Fire

I met a gal on *Match.com*. She had just moved to New York City from California. She was in the travel business and was great looking and smart. We had our first dinner date together at a popular seafood restaurant in the City called the Atlantic Grill, and during the meal our conversation was never at a loss because we had so much to talk about. Between her travel stories and mine, we completely lost track of time and closed the place down at midnight. Overall, it was a great first date.

We talked on the phone during the week and Tracy decided that for our second date she would cook dinner for me at her apartment. She said since she had just moved in, the place might not be the tidiest, but thought since I had told her I didn't cook for myself, she would show me her culinary skills with a nice home cooked meal. We scheduled the date for the following Saturday night. I was not only looking forward to seeing Tracy again, but also to the home cooked meal.

I stopped off to get a bottle of wine and grabbed a taxi to Tracy's apartment. When I got there the doorman told me that she was expecting me and I headed up on the elevator. When I got to her floor, I began looking for her apartment number. I literally saw smoke coming from under the bottom of a door down the hallway and it was her place. I quickly rang the doorbell and when Tracy opened the door, she was frantic. She said her kitchen was on fire. I could see heavy smoke coming from her oven as I raced into the kitchen. When I opened the oven door, flames were shooting out from it. Tracy called down to the doorman while I searched for a fire extinguisher. I found one next to the refrigerator and without even reading the directions, blasted the flames with what looked like shaving cream.

In just seconds the fire was out, but whatever meat she had been cooking didn't look very appetizing. It was ruined of course and Tracy was rattled over the whole thing. Just as I was about to console her by insisting that everything was fine now and that no major damage was done, the fire alarm in the building went off. I'm not sure whether the doorman set it off or a neighbor smelling smoke pushed the panic button, but now we were listening to a loud speaker voice instructing everyone to evacuate the building immediately. Further, it repeated again and again, "Do not use the elevator!"

Tracy called the doorman and told him that the fire was out, but apparently there wasn't anything he could do to cancel the alarm or stop the full evacuation of the building. The fire department was already on its way. Tracy and I looked at each other in disbelief. We weren't really sure whether to walk down the stairs as the blaring loudspeaker continued instructing or not. We were on the fifteenth floor and that was going to be a long walk down many flights of stairs. We decided not to abandon the ship since we knew there was no fire danger.

Suddenly there were firemen with axes in hand storming the hallway outside Tracy's door. I quickly diffused their concerns by telling them the fire was out and inviting them into her unit to check for themselves. When the chief examined the oven, he pulled the grilling pan out and showed us what had happened. Since the stove was new, there was a plastic sheet under the grilling pan that should have been removed before use. That's what had melted and burned causing all the black smoke.

Tracy was very embarrassed about the entire situation. She thanked the firemen for coming and I'm not sure if the tears running down her face at that point were pouring out from emotion or from the smoke. It didn't matter. I gave her a big reassuring hug and it seemed to help. We opened all the windows in her place and fanned the air until it was clear again. She apologized over and again for the catastrophe and ruined dinner, but I insisted we should just get our jackets on and go grab some dinner elsewhere.

Once downstairs, we hailed a cab and I instructed the driver to take us to the Atlantic Grille. I told Tracy we needed a sure thing, and since we had already had a great experience there on our first date, we should go again. So we did. She put her hands over her face and said, "I will never cook again."

We dated for years after that fiasco, and Tracy stayed true to her word. She still hasn't cooked me a dinner.

"The Good With The Bad"

Something For Everyone

There is a dating website that specializes in mutually beneficial relationships and arrangements. In fact, the girls who sign up on it call themselves Sugar Babies. They are women who are students, artists, actresses and models and believe they deserve to date someone who will pamper them, empower them mentally and emotionally, and support them financially in return for dinner dates, company functions and companionship. It sounds like an escort service, but there is never any mention of sex on the site.

What I find most unique about this service is that unlike the traditional dating sites that cater to singles looking for true love, this one doesn't go after that market. This one attracts singles who are looking for anything but the ordinary. In fact, I think I just created a new slogan for them: Anything but the ordinary!

I can't say what the guys on this site offer since I haven't studied the male profiles, but I can tell you that if you're looking for something other than a female sexual companion (remember, they don't mention that three letter word), it can be found on this site. I'll give you a few examples.

One day I had the following types of women respond to me after I wrote in my profile that I was looking for something that wasn't "vanilla". I got five transsexuals and two transgendered women. A few of them were pre-op, several were post-op and the rest were cross-dressers. I had messages from three dominatrices, though they didn't directly refer to themselves by that name, and one said she could be my mistress. One was a part time dominatrix and another one said she liked to give men pain in their testicular area. Dang! Who'd get a thrill out of getting kicked in the groin? Sure, I've had women break my balls, so to speak, but that is a totally different thing.

I also got responses from two young girls who told me they would act as my slutty daughters. Now even though I don't have a daughter myself, I can imagine how a proud father would feel if he knew his girls were selling themselves out as sluts. Then I had an adult film star message me repeatedly and a lesbian couple who were offering friendship.

I don't want to give the impression that ALL the girls on this site are something other than just nice normal girls because I did find one attractive nurse, a school teacher and even a MILF who was in her mid-seventies. Maybe I'm just getting too old to date or I'm looking in the wrong places, but I'm pretty sure my perfect woman won't be found here.

Take-Away: *Variety is the spice of life. It may not be for everyone, but may appeal to many.*

Female Supremacy

I've been on a dating site lately that specializes in arrangements. It features beautiful women who are looking for men not interested in making serious commitments with their personal lives. In exchange for companionship, an arrangement is negotiated. The details of the arrangement can include anything both parties agree to in exchange for an amount of money paid to the woman for that companionship.

I must say, I've never come across an arrangement like the one proposed by a beautiful Russian girl named Natasha. She had a great profile, beautiful pictures and a tagline below her name, which said, "Looking for a unique arrangement?" That got my attention, and my curiosity took me over.

I met Natasha over dinner one evening and she wasted no time in telling me what she was offering. Not only did I find her captivating in appearance, but her command of our conversation kept me glued to attention. She outlined her proposal by starting with a description of her personality and then her philosophy. She said she considered herself to be unique and guaranteed that because of that quality, I would receive much more from the arrangement than just the usual "girlfriend" experience. She explained that she and her girlfriends in Russia believed that our society would be better off if women were in charge. "Men only want one thing from women and one thing only," she barked in Russian style. "Furthermore, they think with their head. The problem is they think with the wrong one."

At that point I wasn't sure whether to continue to hear about Natasha's outlook on life or to run as fast as I could. I curiously and courageously hung in there. I had never met a woman who had an opinion like this before, much less willing to share it with a man.

Natasha continued to explain. "You see, Dan, I am a firm believer in female supremacy, all things feminine. I have come to understand that males gain an invaluable inner focus when their social urges are suppressed. Therefore, here's what I'm offering. I will lock you up for thirty days. There is a chastity device that goes over your "manhood" and although you will be able to do your bodily functions, it will not allow you to masturbate or engage in sexual activity. If you can go thirty days without sex, then I will entertain committing to a monogamous arrangement with you. By doing this for me, we will get to know each other and build a strong foundation. By taking sex out of the equation, your mindset and passion will be redirected, which is extremely beneficial to your self-development as a man. You will become a better man. Whether we end up in a relationship or not, your attitude toward women will be changed because you will no longer see women as just sexual objects. You will respect and appreciate them for everything they stand for in a nonsexual way. "

"Right," I say. "And what happens at the end of thirty days? Do you release me from my sexual imprisonment?"

"We have to wait and see," she answers. "If I feel that you've been trained effectively, the answer is yes. If I feel that you need more training to increase your level of appreciation for women, we will extend your commitment for an additional thirty days. If you break the first commitment or required second one, there will be a release fee of $2,500.00. Do you have any questions? "

Do I have any questions? I'm thinking to myself I sure do, and the first question I'd like answered is whether or not she's ever been locked up before, and I don't mean in a device, I mean in an institution? The second question would be whether anyone ever let her do this to them and if so, are they still alive? But, using my better judgment, I opted not to ask Natasha the questions. Instead, I told her I would really have to think it through and get back to her the following week. My gut was screaming, "If she really believes in female supremacy, she'll keep you locked up forever!"

I never got back to Natasha and then, about two weeks later, she sent me a text that said, "Just as I thought, another guy with no balls ." She obviously didn't realize that the main reason I didn't call her again was so that I could keep my balls.

Take-Away: You can find every type of diversion and perversion online. What is taboo today could be a trend tomorrow. Perfect example, Shades of Grey. Do not experiment with anyone you're not comfortable with. Get to know them first. Do not jump into anything that you're uncomfortable with, and don't be pressured into doing something that you know is wrong for you. If you need to trust anyone, trust yourself and your own instincts.

My Daddy, My Pimp

I met a very interesting girl on a website known as *What's Your Price*. This site specializes for the most part in young women who are willing to date older gentlemen for a price. The price is prearranged can be anywhere from $100 to $500. I've gone out with several women from the site.

I use the site because I travel frequently and want to have someone to dine with while I am away from home and in an unfamiliar city. Although it costs me a hefty sum for the dinner and date, it's been worth it for the companionship. And you should know, these women are not prostitutes as some people may imagine. My experience has been that they are very enjoyable dinner guests and always full of interesting conversation. I will admit, though, they dress super sexy for their dates and that's something we older guys enjoy looking at. At the end of dinner, we both go our separate ways without any hint of sexual favors. OK, maybe a hint or two. I've exchanged phone numbers on two different occasions because the gals were so enjoyable to dine with. Honestly, it has nothing to do with me wanting a hooker for the night.

What has been a curiosity for me has been to discover the types of girls who post their profiles on this site and the reasons why. This is the story about one of them.

Mia was a small, petite girl who was extremely pretty. The first time I met her was at a café in Fort Lauderdale. She was dressed super sexy in tight black slacks and a black embroidered halter top that broadcast her magnificent cleavage. It was a beautiful sight. I thought she was just gorgeous.

As we were eating dinner, I asked Mia if she had been on the site a long time and how she found out about it. She explained that her father actually told her about it a year earlier. She said that she lived with her dad because he was very ill and dying of cancer. She said he had been a smoker his whole life and even though he was chronically ill, he still smoked more than five packs of cigarettes a day. He thought it would be a good way for Mia to meet guys because she wasn't getting out of the house for fun or any social interaction. He didn't want to burden her so heavily with his condition.

As I was listening to Mia explain the story, I thought it was interesting. Then she went on to tell the rest of the story. While she is at work during the day, her father sets her dating schedule and negotiates the prices with potential suitors, fictitiously presenting himself as Mia while texting the interested men. I thought about my first texts with "Mia" when I found her profile. I had originally offered $100 for her time to meet me for dinner. "Mia" drove a hard bargain in those negotiations and I ended up paying $150 for the date with her. Little did I know it was her dying dad who was actually handling the art of the deal!

Mia then goes on to tell me that she gives her dad half the money for any of the dates he negotiates!

I don't know about you, but in my book that looks a little like daddy pimping, although I didn't say that to Mia. I asked her why he needs to make money that way and she said he needed it to support his nicotine and gambling addictions. He goes to a nearby casino every day. I suppose the look on my face dropped when she told me that because she quickly added, "Really, it's a win/win/win arrangement for everybody. My dad's happy, I'm happy and the gentlemen who I date are happy. I provide interesting conversation and eye appeal for my dates to enjoy, don't I?"

I couldn't disagree.

As I drove home that first night after hearing Mia's story, I realized that she was saying everything possible to justify the "pimping" arrangement she had with her dad. She couldn't honestly believe what they were doing was right, could she? I understand there's nothing illegal going on because she's not having sex with anyone, but somehow it just doesn't seem right. It's wrong. Yes, it's very wrong, but will that stop me from seeing Mia again?

Nope. We've gone out several more times since our initial date, and I still enjoy her company. And why shouldn't I? It's a win/win/win. She's getting out of the house for some social time, I get companionship and most importantly, it's making her dying daddy very happy!

Will Work For Boobs

On the *What's Your Price* dating site, a person can offer young sexy girls money in return for their companionship. A lot of people may think this site is an escort service, but it's not. Believe me, I've dated many girls from this site and there was never any talk about sexual favors. I've told one story about a girl I met on WYP where the young woman gave half of her money to her father for his gambling and smoking habits. This is another story about a girl I met on the same site.

One evening I took Lori to one of my favorite waterfront restaurants in Fort Lauderdale, the Charthouse. I had negotiated a fee of $125 for her dinner companionship. If you think about it, it's a great deal for Lori. She not only makes money for being with me, but gets to enjoy an excellent meal in a beautiful and relaxing atmosphere. It's a great deal for me also because I get great food, look at amazing boats go by, and have a beautiful woman to dine with. Lori didn't disappoint in the beauty category at all. Her looks reminded me of Kate Hudson. She was wearing a shorty-short skirt, six inch stiletto heels and a corset top that pushed her boobs up, accentuating a nice cleavage. Yes, we guys do enjoy looking at things like that.

Our dinner was great. Lori had steak and lobster. I had prime rib, and together we finished two bottles of wine. Lori was a little drunk by then and somehow our conversation turned to her reasons for being on WYP. She started rambling a bit about what a great body she had, shapely and fit, and how confident she was in her own skin, except for one thing. She was insecure about her breast size. With that, she pulled her corset down and showed me her boobs. She flashed me right then and there, but thank goodness the room was dark and most customers had already left by this time. Something like that would have really been embarrassing had others been around.

So Lori went on to explain that she makes between $500 and $600 a week going out on dates from the WYP site. She figured that in two more months, she would have collected enough money to get the boob job that she really wanted. I told her that I thought her boobs looked great just as they were, but she disagreed. She insisted that either d-size or double d's would make her much happier. Who was I to argue. She had already thought the whole thing through, and knew that with larger boobs, she would be in even greater demand on the site. With the bigger boobs, she could negotiate in the $200 and up range for her companionship, instead of a paltry $100. I don't know if that wine was getting to my brain by then too, but what she said was beginning to make complete business sense to me. To her credit, I could see an enterprising spirit in her.

I'm not sure that her online dating business plan would hold much water with an investment banker if she ever needed a loan, but I definitely appreciate her entrepreneurial mentality. I have no doubt that she has a great online dating future and will be a very successful young lady whatever she sets her mind or body to.

Lactate Tolerance

There is an online dating site that specializes in young ladies, called Sugar Babies, who are looking for a gentleman, known as a Sugar Daddy, to help them financially. Most of these women are still in school and need help with tuition. Many of them are single moms who are struggling financially and looking for extra income to raise their child or children. Then there are also some who are just living on their own and need help in paying their everyday bills. The site makes no mention of sexual favors being offered and although it might be assumed, there are no promises made. Many of the profiles, however, end with the language "I know how to please a man in return" so judge for yourself on what that means.

Looking through the profiles, I would say there are literally hundreds of women on this site looking for wealthy and powerful men to connect with. They seem to compete with each other for attention. Each Sugar Baby tries to offer something that the others don't or can't. Some advertise themselves with modeling looks, some claim to be experts in dominance or submission, and I even found one who was offering something that very few could compete with, breast milk. Yes, you heard me right.

A girl wrote to me. Her name was Bethany. She told me that she loved my profile and that she could offer me something that no other woman could. "Please read my profile and see if you might be ready to explore the wild side with a naughty little mommy." I immediately looked at Bethany's narrative in her profile. It said, "Just a sweet young thing looking for a guy. Now the bonus with me. If you love large breasts, then you'll love me. I have large cones with puffy nipples and I lactate if you're into that sort of thing. I'm also into several other fetishes." She goes on to say that her Sugar Daddy won't be disappointed in this hot momma and wants to give her attention to just one lucky guy.

I responded to Bethany and told her that I was really new to the fetish thing and that dating a much younger girl was probably my biggest diversion, or perversion depending on what you believe. Bethany convinced me to keep an open mind and said she was a big believer in not knocking something until you've tried it. I loved her personality. She looked and appeared so innocent, but I discovered pretty quickly that deep down inside she was a very naughty girl.

I made a date with Bethany and we've been together for several months now. I adore her! I won't say which fetishes of hers I enjoy and which ones are not for me, but she has definitely made me feel like a new man. I feel younger and more virile than ever. Okay, I admit this too. I am also a wee bit more perverted than I used to be.

Thanks to this online site and thanks to my new Sugar Baby.

Take-Away: *"Don't knock something till you try it". Be careful and keep your guard up at all times.*

A Strange Profession

I met a very attractive woman on *Match.com* recently. She was not only pretty, but well educated too. She had a couple of children and posted numerous pictures of herself, which portrayed her to be an All-American girl and mother. We talked on the phone and decided to meet at one of my favorite Fort Lauderdale cafes across the water. Her name was Rachel.

In person, Rachel looked exactly like her photos, which is an unusual thing in the world of internet dating. You never know who or what you're going to get because most photos are a tad deceptive (intentionally or not). But Rachel's were true to life. She had the most beautiful green eyes, jet black hair and long slender legs. We had a warm greeting and ordered up some drinks and appetizers right away. The evening seemed to fly by, which is not always the case when I meet someone the first time. More than once I've been stuck with a date who made conversation like pulling teeth. Rachel wasn't at all like that. She couldn't stop talking the whole evening nor could I. I was fascinated with the subject of our conversation.

Early on in the evening I had asked Rachel what she did for a living. She danced around the question for a bit and then answered, "I humiliate men for a living."

"Excuse me?"

She laughed and repeated herself, "I humiliate men for a living."

Now that I was sure I'd heard her correctly, I smiled and said, "don't most married women eventually turn to that profession as well?"

We had a good laugh over my sarcastic comment, and she then assured me she wasn't kidding. Humiliating men was her profession. She began to explain more about how she made her living humiliating men, a skill she performs both publicly and privately for her clients. She had my undivided attention. This was a new one on me.

Please understand, I'm not naïve. I've been around the old block a few times in my life as a bachelor and I know about underground societies of professionals, like myself, who are into many types of fetishes such as domination, S & M and things of that kinky sort. What I didn't know, however, was that since the novel *Shades of Grey* surfaced as Main Street reading, that alternative lifestyle has become an even larger marketplace of people who have "outed" themselves. Rachel explained that she has simply taken advantage of this increased market demand. It's all legal, she explained, and she participates in no sexual activities with her clients. Her work is completely above board and she said she makes a lot of money doing it.

I was fascinated with Rachel's description of her work. In fact I don't remember ever a time that someone's profession got my attention like this. Rachel went on to explain that the art of humiliation involved specific tasks that she masterfully carried out for her client. Sometimes the tasks were performed in private, but usually they were carried out for other's to see. I'm sure like me, you'd be interested in some examples. She told me story after story.

A Strange Profession

Many of the clients prefer public humiliations where it appears that they are being controlled and put down by Rachel, subtle things like bowing to light her cigarette or walking a pace behind while she is shopping (using the client's credit card of course) and then carrying her purchases like a peon of some sort. In private settings, many clients like her to make them give her a massage or pedicure. One paid her to allow him to prepare a home cooked meal and then eat his food from a dog bowl on the floor next to her feet. You get the picture?

I was amazed and what was hard to believe, but true, was that these were all clients of professional standing, high powered people, CEOs of major firms, bank executives, Wall Street guys, attorneys and doctors. She had me mesmerized the entire evening with her stories and candidly answered every one of my questions about the details of each one. What a fascinating open book of a night!

When the waiter interrupted a particularly interesting story she was telling, I suddenly realized the restaurant had emptied out and we were the last people there. I had been captivated for three hours, but it was time to go. I kissed her goodnight and agreed we'd have to get together again soon. As I drove home that night, I felt like I wanted to see her again but decided it wouldn't be possible to date a woman like Rachel who was probably seeing twenty-five other guys a week on a professional basis and knowing what she did with them. I decided the only way a relationship with her could work would be if I became one of her clients. On second thought, why would I have to pay to be humiliated? That reminds me. I need to call my ex.

Fit To Be Tied

I met a great gal online. We had been out together several times before I invited her one Saturday night to my townhouse to watch the NCAA Final Four on my big screen. We were kicked back eating pizza and drinking beer when my doorbell rang. It was my buddy Lewis who lived next door. I suppose since he saw my car parked in the garage, he figured I was home alone. I waived him in the door and told him to help himself to the pizzas that were still steamy hot and sitting on the coffee table.

Just about then my phone rang so I went to the kitchen to take the call and get a cold beer for Lewis. The call was from a friend confirming our golf game next morning and once that was settled, I headed back to the den. Rebecca and Lewis were sitting side-by-side on the couch and quite to my surprise, they had just lit up a joint to smoke.

"Hey, you two got to know each other awfully quick!"

I took a toke myself and settled in to watch the game.

At half time, Rebecca got up to take the dishes to the kitchen and trash the empty beer bottles sitting around. She said she was still hungry and I realized she had the munchies from smoking weed. She craved Haagen-Dazs Chocolate Chocolate Chip ice cream. So being a gracious host, I agreed to make a quick run to the store for halftime.

I couldn't have been gone for more than ten minutes, maybe fifteen, and when I walked back in my house there was no sign of Rebecca or Lewis. I called out for them and Lewis hollered back from upstairs. *What the hell are they doing upstairs?* I wondered.

"Whoa! Whoa!" was all that came out of my mouth when I looked into my bedroom. Rebecca was dressed in nothing but her panties and bra. She was tied to my bed with what looked like several of my neckties. She had something stuffed in her mouth that I was pretty sure looked like my rolled up golf socks. "Whoa! Are you guys out of your f…. mind? What the hell are you doing?"

Lewis started babbling something about Rebecca being so stoned and wanting to fulfill one of her fantasies. He went on saying that she asked him to tie her up and gag her, and then he was supposed to scare her with the threat of rape. Well even as high as I was from the pot, I knew this was playing a risky little game. Plus, I couldn't believe my date, who I hardly even knew, was tied to my bed, spread-eagle with my friend and neighbor threatening to rape her.

I came unglued. "Untie her now!"

Rebecca saw how angry I was and spit the sock gag out of her mouth. She started apologizing and taking full blame for the situation. She insisted she made Lewis do it. And Lewis, what a big dumb oaf! I took that idiot aside and reamed him out. "Did you think about the repercussions of what could happen to both of us if Rebecca realizes after her buzz fades that she never wanted you to tie her up? We'd both go to jail!!!!"

I was so angry I could hardly see straight, and honestly, looking back at it, I don't think Lewis had a clue of what I was talking about. After all, there was no doubt Rebecca wanted what was going on in the bedroom. There was no force involved, but whether there was or not, it doesn't matter because I didn't want that going on in my house under any circumstances. Rebecca, still in her bra and panties, stumbled her way back downstairs to the den and Lewis went home.

Rebecca and I ended up falling asleep on the couch that night, and then spent the next two days together at my place.

I am here to tell you, this was some crazy chick I had met online. She was the wildest and kinkiest girl I had ever dated, and as it turned out, we ended up dating for almost a year after that incident. I had never considered myself to be a kinky dude, but after hanging with Rebecca, I have discovered a whole new world! She gave new meaning to March Madness.

His Sexy Beard

Talk about finding a cushiony job! Let me tell you. I had been out of work for several weeks and running out of money fast. One of my girlfriends told me about a dating site she was on that specialized in men paying for companionship and friendship of women. She assured me it wasn't anything like escorting, and I might even find the man of my dreams while getting paid for my search. I was fast approaching financial desperation so I thought I'd give it a try.

I filled out a brief profile and posted a few pictures. My girlfriend helped me with what to say and although I wasn't sure which photos of myself were appropriate, she gave me a confident push based on her experience. Since I work out daily at a gym and have a terrific body, we decided my Spandex outfits would show me with my best foot forward. I also added one picture of myself wearing a formal gown and another where I am on the beach in a skimpy bikini. I cast my net out.

Lo and behold! I caught something. I actually caught a whole net full by the next morning, but there was one fish-guy who stood out from the pile. He was pictured standing next to a boat with one hand over his brow as if looking at the sea. He had a neatly trimmed beard and mustache that gave him a mature sex appeal, and reminded me of the Most Interesting Man in the Dos XXX beer commercial. His headline said, "I'm looking for my

First Mate." I thought his sense of humor was cute and the boat looked impressive too so I responded to his mail.

Mark lived fairly close to me and we arranged to meet for dinner the very next night. He pulled up in his fancy European car that was either a Ferrari or Maserati. Either way, it was one of those midlife crisis automobiles that wealthy men buy. He was just as handsome and physically fit as his photo showed him to be and had a full head of hair, which met the basic qualifications I was looking for. We had an enjoyable dinner and found that we had a lot in common. It was quite a coincidence that he knew a good friend of mine named Tina and also hung out at several of the same bars and restaurants as us. I kept thinking he looked familiar, but wasn't sure and couldn't place having ever met him before so I didn't trouble myself over the thought any further. I just flowed with the dinner conversation and laughter. By the end of the evening I felt the date had gone well.

The following weekend Mark invited me to his boat for cocktails and told me to bring my girlfriend Tina along. He said we would all go to dinner afterwards. Tina and I arrived at the dock on schedule and found his boat with no problem. Of all the gorgeous boats docked at the marina, Mark's was the biggest. We were warmly welcomed aboard and mingled with his other guests, enjoying drinks and amazing appetizers. Shortly after dark and seeing his guests off, Mark led Tina and I to his car parked at the gangway entrance. This time he was driving a Bentley, and now I was really getting the picture of his extravagant lifestyle. I felt like arm candy getting out in front of the restaurant. There were people who turned and stared as we waltzed our way into the front lobby.

It was an excellent Italian dinner and the conversation was lively and fun. Then Mark took us back to his boat where we had after dinner drinks before Tina and I headed for home. I confided in Tina that I felt very comfortable with Mark already and Tina agreed that she could see a good connection between the two of us, but added that there was something I should know about him. I frowned because her tone didn't sound positive. She said she thought he might be a player for the other team. I was a little surprised by her comment, but then had to admit I had also noticed a few small personality traits that might have been revealing. I didn't want to believe it though.

Mark took me for dinner the following week and during our meal told me that he had a job proposition for me. He said he was going to be taking the boat to the Bahamas the following week for business and would be gone for about a month. He said there would be various clients coming aboard during that time that he would be entertaining and would like my companionship. I asked him what my duties would be and he said all I needed to do was to look beautiful each day. He said I should bring plenty of bathing suits, short sexy dresses and little beach-type outfits and that I would be introduced as his girlfriend. He added that although he would like me to sleep in the stateroom with him, sex wasn't required or expected. And, oh yea, the best part was that he was going to pay me $2,000 per week.

I've been with Mark now for two months and we have been away for most of the summer aboard his boat. I can't believe my luck. He actually pays me to sit out and tan, his crew caters to me like a princess and he has been a perfect gentleman. Other than a little cuddle and kiss we've had no sexual intercourse, which is fine with me. I can't believe my luck in finding Mark online and although I don't know how long this journey will last, I can certainly see why they named this little island we're at now Paradise Island. It's been nothing but.

Like A Good Neighbor

I broke up with my boyfriend Chuck, bringing an end to our five year dating relationship. Although I had seen the end coming for over a year, I hung in there because our connection was convenient and familiar. Both of us lived in Chicago, had some mutual friends and knew each other's families. Furthermore, I really didn't want to be single again. But I knew going our separate ways was the best for both of us so I made the difficult break and now it's done.

It's been about six months since then and I haven't been dating much. Although my friends have been trying to fix me up with someone each week, nothing has clicked. It's not that I'm not ready or that I'm still hung up over Chuck, there just hasn't been a connection that interested me in pursuing so I decided to take matters into my own hands. I signed up on *Match.com*.

After ruminating for an hour, over which of my pictures to post on the site and filling out the tedious profile, I got approved. Email messages started pouring in. This tickled my fancy and before I knew it I had a hundred possibilities to pick from. Granted, they weren't all tall, dark and handsome gentlemen, and I have to say that not all of them were even gentlemen. There were definitely some crude and obscene photos sent my way, but at least I had lots of options I could take or leave. As for the crude- dudes, I have to say nothing surprises me anymore.

So I set up several dates with guys for drinks at a local restaurant near me called Gibson's. They were all nice guys, just not for me. Then I lucked out and met a guy named Billy. He was a tall, dark and handsome man. He was funny, sincere and, I think, rich. I say rich because I found out that he lived in the same swanky condo building as my former boyfriend Chuck, which was quite a coincidence I thought. Fortunately, that particular building is huge so I figured the chances of ever running into Chuck would be minimal. Besides, I had moved on from that old relationship and felt sure Chuck had to. So what the heck!

At any rate, Billy and I continued to date. We were getting along famously and had a lot in common. We had similar tastes in food and even discovered we had the same favorite restaurant, Joe's Stone Crab and Steakhouse. Billy took me there twice in the past three weeks.

The other night after dinner there, Billy asked if I would like to go back to his place with him. Since he had been the perfect gentleman thus far, I told him I'd love to. We strolled down Michigan Avenue and into his beautiful building. I knew that the doorman in the lobby recognized me, but thank God he had the good sense not to say my name or give any indication to Billy that he knew me to have been a regular in that building over the past years. We were whisked up the high-speed elevator to William's floor.

On the way up I was so preoccupied with Billy's playful tickling and hugging, I hadn't paid any attention to the floor number he pushed. Well, *de'ja' vu*! When the elevator doors opened, I was on Chuck's floor. Not only were we on Chuck's floor, but Billy then lead me into his apartment, which was situated directly opposite Chuck's. Awkward! I wasn't sure whether I should say anything to Billy or not. I didn't want to ruin the mood so I said nothing.

I ended up spending that night with Billy, and when I left the next morning, I was so nervous before finally getting out of the building. With my luck, I feared I'd run right into my old ex and what an embarrassing situation that would be, not that I really had any reason to be embarrassed. I just didn't know how Chuck might react to me dating his next door neighbor. The good thing was I didn't bump into him on my way out. The bad thing however was that I knew I had to tell Billy as soon as possible before the doorman spilled the beans. I had a feeling that I was going to be dating Billy for a long time to come. I like him a lot, and I hope he'll be ok with this strange coincidence.

All Choked Up

You asked for my story, so here's the account of my first date with Robert who I met on the internet. We scheduled a dinner date and he arrived on time, looking clean cut and conservatively dressed. After the typical getting to know you chatter on the basics, he opens the door to tell me that he is into kink. In a teasing sort of way I say, "What do you mean?"

He says, "It's best I don't tell you until our second or third date. I don't want to scare you off because I find you to be a gorgeous woman."

With that I am both flattered and intrigued so I say, "Oh, come on. Tell me. You won't scare me off." He says, "No. I like you and want to see you again.

So, I drop the whole thing and we spend the next hour enjoying a lovely dinner. I tell him about my past marriage and he talks casually about his, telling me that he divorced his former wife of ten years because she never wanted to have children. He says he is looking for another long term relationship, and intimates repeatedly that he misses being in a close and trusting relationship with a woman. He says he is a one-woman man.

By now I am feeling attracted to Robert and we take a slow hand-in-hand walk to my car parked in the lot of the restaurant. I'm thinking he's a real gentleman. I get in my car and he leans in to give me a kiss goodnight when all of a sudden both his hands are around my neck. With a tightening grip on my throat, he presses his mouth firmly against my lips. I feel like I'm going to choke. Panicking, I want to scream but can't. Then just as unexpectedly, he eases up and steps back from my car saying, "Sweetheart, I love choking women during sex. It's the most erotic thing in the world."

How's that for an ending of a first date?

I am in shock. I snap, screaming, "You crazy idiot!" and I hit the ignition and lay on the horn as I'm speeding out of the parking lot, my head spinning over what has just happened. As I continue racing toward home the flush begins to leave my face. I feel warm, really warm, in a way I have never felt before. Believe it or not, I can' stop thinking about that kiss.

A text message shows up on my cell phone. It's Robert. He says, "I hope I didn't scare you. I'm sorry if I did."

I take a deep breath and think about it for a few minutes, then text him back, "When do you want to get together again?"

We've been dating for two years now.

The Fake Internet Girlfriend Service

Just when you thought you had heard about every imaginable kind of dating Web site, you can thank Notre Dame linebacker Manti Te'O for yet one more creative site. After the publicity of Manti's lie about a fake online girlfriend, there is now a dating Web site that rents fake internet girlfriends.

For the pricey monthly fee of some $250.00, you can have a fake internet girlfriend. It is a service site with actual women who connect with you on Facebook or any other social networking site. They will post messages to your profile, text you, call while you're in public places and even leave you a voicemail. In fact, your fake girlfriend will text you up to ten times a month and leave up to two telephone messages confirming (fake) dinner plans or leave a message for the purpose of checking on you.

The company behind the site hires actresses to play the girlfriend roles. They can adapt to whatever type of personality the customer desires. They can act the part of a distant but loving girlfriend, social and upbeat, or quirky and misunderstood gal. You could request an obnoxious girlfriend or a real bitch of a mate. (From my experience I wouldn't waste my money on a fake internet "bitch" though because there are plenty of real ones out there for free! Just kidding, ladies.)

It seems that fake partner services have actually existed for some time in Japan. In that country it is not uncommon for Japanese men to rent a best man for their wedding or, due to social pressure, rent a female counterpart to establish an appearance of masculinity when he is yet single. But there are other reasons this service may come in handy. It's ideal for a guy who wants to break up with his girlfriend and needs a creative way to do it. Imagine the soon-to-be-dumped girlfriend who gets a sexy text from another woman who claims to have been sleeping with her man for months. Or what about a guy who needs a sexy girl to make his girlfriend jealous? What about a homosexual who is still in the closet and needs an online girlfriend to trick his family or others into believing that he has a girlfriend?

Take-Away: Services like this don't exist and certainly wouldn't survive if not for consumer demand. Obviously, there is a need in the world for this service. As a matter of fact, there is not only one site like this but several. I can't help feel a little sad though to think someone wants to be loved so desperately that they'd pay for a service that offers nothing but deception. I guess we have to give Manti Te'O the credit for popularizing the concept.

Professional Daters

I've gone out with hundreds of girls during my lifetime and must have spent tens of thousands of dollars entertaining them in one way or another. I've paid for dinners, bought tickets to movies, sporting events, concerts, airline travel, hotels and we won't even begin to talk about outright gifts I've purchased. Yet after all of that dating experience, there was something I never knew about in the dating world until now, Professional Daters.

One of my recent dates, Debra, gave me a good tutorial on these people. She's obviously been tuned into a radio station I missed along the way because "Dating for Dinners" is a song I never heard. It's not really a song, mind you, but she used the phrase like it was some everyday melody as she explained this apparent dating trend. She claims that even on the most basic dating sites girls will go out with guys just for the free dinner. They're girls who don't necessarily want to be in a relationship, despite what their profile might say, and often they are already involved in a relationship. Some are married. And, if you can believe this one, she said some girls eat half their meal and take the other half home with them for their significant other. Who would have thought?

The fact is that these women go out with guys who they have no romantic interest in or physical attraction toward. Their agenda has nothing to do with exploring a possible relationship with the poor sap that's paying the tab. Many are actually narcissistic and have no guilt over their misleading behavior. They just get up every morning wondering what the world will do for them that day. I'm here to tell you, this type of woman is toying with a man's emotions and entertaining her self-centered life in the process. Really not good!

As Debra continued telling me more and more about Professional Daters, I was starting to get a little nauseous. It seemed like every example she told me about was striking a personal chord in my dating memory banks. It got worse. She then explained that the professional dater is really by trade an actress and continually rehearses her role of showing affection to her victim-dates. Some of these women become extremely talented in making their dates believe there is a genuine interest in them when the truth is, they could care less. Debra said these women will sometimes have to force themselves to actually touch the guy. It might be that she places her hand on his during dinner or, more boldly, may slide her hand over his thigh. Any of this sort of touching, you must remember, is nothing more than an act that is intended to make the guy think she likes him. Whether she is subtle or brazen, the bottom line is the same with the professional dater, she's playing him like a fiddle!

Debra said young girls, say under the age of thirty, don't usually play the professional dating game because they still have their youthful advantage. It's the older ones that develop the art and then earn the title Professional Dater. There are some that she has known personally who she claims, if caught on film, would surely be nominated for an Academy Award.

OK, Debra! My faith in the whole online dating scene has now been destroyed. It's like the day I found out Santa Claus didn't exist. Sad, very sad, so Debra tried to assure me that not all women are Professional Daters. She said she certainly wasn't one of them and that she genuinely loved my company, especially my sense of humor. That encouraged me a little and she sweetly took my hand.

When we had finished dinner, I walked Debra to her car. She kissed me goodnight saying she'd see me soon.

The kiss was probably a pity kiss.

Her "goodnight" farewell was no doubt rehearsed.

So, as I drove off alone again I asked myself, "Who do I believe anymore?"

Take-Away: Beware of Professional Daters. Don't let your date pick the restaurant. Often times it will be pricey. Date within your means. Don't date "out of your league."

Beware of Separate Bedrooms

I went on a site recently that specialized in travel dating. It had been featured on the television program *20/20*. Once you sign up on the site, you can then study the profiles and decide who you wish to invite on a vacation. You pay travel expenses and all accommodations for your date just as though they were your boy or girlfriend. The catch is that this date is someone you've never personally met before. Now although you may have texted or had some telephone conversations before the trip arrangements were carved in stone, there is no way to know for certain whether that special chemistry is going to be there until you meet face-to-face. It's a gamble. You have no idea if there will be any lovemaking or whether you are getting stuck with a sourpuss. But for some of us, it's worth the risk. No guts? No glory! No harm, no foul…just lots of money spent.

I met Christie on the site and she looked beautiful and sweet. As if all of them don't? Christie lived in New Jersey, and I invited her to meet me in Las Vegas for a weekend. Christie was young, around twenty-two, and although she was excited about meeting me there, she was skeptical (as she wisely should have been) that I might turn out to be someone different than who I portrayed myself to be. I assured her that I had good intentions. She clarified the expectations by saying she was not agreeing to intimate relations with me unless the right chemistry was there between us. I agreed of course because there is no other right answer from a guy, right? I assured her that I had been brought up with good manners and respect for women. I then offered her the following arrangement: not only would I fly her out to Vegas to stay at a first class hotel, the Bellagio, but I would book a separate room for her. She thought that was the nicest thing anyone had ever offered her. In her mind I had now become her Prince Charming and the perfect gentleman. For the next two weeks, we talked numerous times by phone, and I could tell she was really excited about the trip as she had never been to Vegas before. I could also tell she was excited about meeting me.

Now, everything above is true with regards to me being a perfect gentleman. I was raised well and I wasn't going to expect sex out of her if there was no mutual chemistry. The fact that I had booked a separate room for her was probably going to cost me another $1,000 for the weekend, but I thought it was the only way a gentleman could put her worries to bed…rest, I mean.

I learned from other women on this site that a guy offering a girl her own room and actually booking it for her upon arrival is not really so smart if you're the girl because it creates a false sense of security. Think about it. The guy who booked the room can get a key to the room later if he wants. The guy booking the room can limit any or all charges the gal might try to run up while staying in the room. Ultimately, as long as the room is in his name and he is paying for it, he has complete control. He could even lock his date out of her room if he wanted and she'd be stranded. Other stories women from this site told me about were of men who got women drunk or slipped something in their drink and then took advantage of them, and that these kinds of incidents aren't typically reported by the humiliated women.

Well, lucky for Christie that I'm not one of those kinds of men. I didn't tell her any of these foreboding tales before the trip because I was sincerely trying to make her feel comfortable and safe. I did plan to talk to her about these risks though once we met and she was comfortable with me.

So how should women handle the separate bedroom issue when travel dating? It seems to me the safest way is for them to get their own room and ask the guy to reimburse the expense at the beginning of the trip. Remember, if the date doesn't go well or there's no chemistry, the lady may not get reimbursed afterwards. She'd be running high risk of his refusal to pay because a frustrated and disappointed guy is generally not too congenial.

But, the good travel dating report is that Christie and I did hit if off together, and I was able to cancel the extra room after the first night we were in Vegas. It's fair to say we had instant chemistry when we finally met face-to-face. We had a great time drinking, eating, gambling and seeing her favorite singer, Celine Dion. Christie was like a kid in the candy store, and I wrapped the weekend up by treating her to a rather generous shopping trip before we boarded our flights for home. We've kept our relationship going and even took a cruise to the Caribbean together which was fantastic.

Take-Away: There are good guys out there and some bad ones, and ladies need to protect themselves in every way especially when travel dating. Meeting your travel companion face-to-face before showing up for a blind mini-vacation date is good advice! Although geographic challenges may exist, it really is the prudent thing to do. And again, get your own room in your own name. This, too, is the prudent thing to do.

Beware of Separate Bathrooms

Over the years I've had women ask for separate bedrooms when we went out of town on a date, especially if we hadn't known each other long. I understand that. But Sheila, a girl I met on *Match.com* and have dated for over a year still insists on separate bathrooms when we travel. Now that may seem like a little thing to accommodate, but let me tell you the reality of it. Hotel rooms don't have two bathrooms. One bedroom suites don't have two full bathrooms. So, wherever we go my hotel bill is double because I have to book two rooms. And since we stay at fairly expensive places, this two bathroom luxury has been costing me thousands of dollars.

Are you wondering why my girlfriend insists on having her own bathroom? I'll tell you. First of all, she's twenty years older than me and although she still looks sensational, I think it must take a lot of extra doing to make herself look sensational from head to toe. I'm considering all facets from clothing to makeup and hair. It a time consuming job she works on in there, and there are obviously some secret tricks and cosmetic items she doesn't want me to see. But then there are things I don't want her to see of mine either. I use Rogaine for my hair and want to keep my Viagra an undercover secret, so I do understand the privacy thing. I've always honored my commitment to not use her bathroom, however I did peak inside one time when she wasn't around and she'd left the door ajar. There were more cosmetics and hair pieces in there than Macy's displays on their counters at Christmas. There were bottles and jars, brushes and tools and frankly, it reminded me of some sort of scientific laboratory.

Now back to my problem at hand, the expense of two bathrooms. I'm thinking this could be one solution. I'm thinking maybe I could start taking my showers in the health club facilities, which most hotels have. I've done that before after a workout even when I had my own room with bath. I could pee in the lobby restroom when I have to get up in the middle of the night too. Heck, the advantage with that is that no one would be around to notice me down there in my pajamas at say 3:00 a.m. There wouldn't be a creature stirring, not even a mouse! But, then that would be pretty inconvenient if our room was on the twentieth floor.

How did I handle the bathroom problem in the past when our hotel was booked up and they only had one room left? That actually happened once and I had to get a room at a hotel next door just so Sheila could have her own bathroom. That wasn't a good experience for me though. It was the middle of summer and by the time I ran across the street back to Sheila's hotel I was so sweaty I needed another shower. That was completely impractical.

Oh the things we do for love! I think I'll keep on booking two rooms though, always in advance, because I'd much rather pay for the separate bathroom Sheila wants than end up in a separate bedroom from her.

The Girl With Too Much Baggage

I was anxious to get away for a vacation and wanted a radical change of scenery, so I decided on a six-day trip to Las Vegas over the Memorial Day holiday. I had been cultivating a relationship on my dating site with two different ladies for some time and decided to first invite Gracie to join me there for a couple of days. After discussing the details of my invitation, she agreed to the blind date. I booked my flight from Florida, made hotel reservations at the Wynn and paid for her $600.00 roundtrip airline ticket from O'Hare to Vegas. The plan was now carved in stone for our get-together in two weeks.

Gracie's photos in her bio were gorgeous. Those images were vividly swirling around in my head as I waited for her to step off her flight in Vegas when that Friday morning finally arrived. Since my flight landed twenty minutes early, I paced the corridor in the terminal like an expectant father-in-waiting. I downed two Manhattans at the bar to calm myself, but my anticipation of our first face-to-face meeting only grew larger when I saw that her plane would be landing late. Believe me, this sort of thing is hard on a guy.

Finally, Flight 680 was deplaning. Trying to look cool, calm and handsome, I stood with my arms crossed and casually leaned against a post at her gate with all my hidden expectations waiting to be fulfilled by the sight of that gorgeous body and inviting smile. So wouldn't you know, from behind my shoulder I heard someone say, "Hey, you." It was my blind date, Gracie. I had no idea who she was at first because this woman didn't look anything like the images on the website. What was obviously a fantasy illusion of her in my mind, suddenly disappeared. My morale took a dive.

But, being the gentleman that I am, I greeted her warmly and we proceeded to the baggage claim area. She pointed out her suitcase on the conveyer and I hoisted it to the floor with the help of a man standing nearby. It was the size of a trunk and must have weighed a hundred pounds. It was the only suitcase I have ever seen that didn't have roller wheels on it, so I smartly went to get a luggage cart rather than risk breaking my back hauling it curbside. Just when I figured we were good to go, she informed me that she still had another bag coming around. This one was smaller but weighed about two hundred pounds. Onto the cart it went with the help of two other men standing beside me. And if that wasn't enough to annoy me to the brink, she said, "Wait. Here comes the last one."

This woman had three giant suitcases and a carryon of her belongings for a three day date with me. If I told you she was going on a four week cruise, I'd have said it was too much luggage!

We loaded into our cab and I took a brief sigh of relief from the baggage fiasco when she then handed me a piece of paper from her pocket. It was a receipt for $238.00, and she asked if I would reimburse her now for the airline's extra baggage charges. Already annoyed from her counterfeit website photos and ridiculous cargo of baggage, I thought her demand for payment was as bad as it could get. It wasn't.

My very, very bad decision to put her name on my hotel room gave her charging privileges on my account there. From the minute she arrived until the minute she left, she charged breakfast, lunch and late night dinner through room service, not to mention at least ten drinks a day around the pool and two spa treatments. The killer was when I said goodbye to her three days later as her bags were loaded into the cab to deliver her back to the airport. It was the final nail in my coffin when she asked me to give her another $238.00 to get her extra and overweight baggage back to Chicago!

Days later when I returned home to Florida, my buddy asked me if I won in Vegas. I said, "I got lucky. I broke even."

***Take-Away:** Guys, don't let women take advantage of your kindness. Paying $500 for excessive baggage is crazy. But then again, the fact that your date brought her an entire wardrobe on a weekend getaway should have been your clue as to her mental state of mind. Maybe she was intending to come home with you after the trip. Possibly move-in, which in this case, I later found that this was her intention.*

The Girl With Not Enough Baggage

All was not lost because I still had three days of vacation in beautiful Las Vegas and my second lady from the website was scheduled to arrive thirty minutes before Gracie's flight was to depart. Who knows, the two women might have passed each other in the terminal!

Kathy's arrangements were to take a cab from the airport and meet me in the lobby of the Wynn. I was trying to stay optimistic about my second blind date and avoided dwelling on any mental images of her since I had just learned that lesson so well with Gracie. But she turned out to be an unexpected surprise when we met. She was actually prettier than her website photos. She took nothing for granted. She charged nothing and brought with her an overnight bag and small suitcase - one with rollers, I might add. There really is a God!

As I carried her little suitcase and garment bag up to the room, I said to her, "Do you have anything in here because it feels empty?"

Her reply was, "Just the essentials: bathing suit, lingerie, little black dress and my toothbrush."

Two sides to every coin. Viva Las Vegas! It would have been a horrible trip if I hadn't plotted -oops - planned for backup arrangements on my vacation. Talk about making lemonade out of lemons.

Little Italy...Little In Common

I met a young lady online and we agreed to get together one beautiful weekend afternoon at a small Italian restaurant in Little Italy. I believe the name of the place was Costa Azurra. I ordered a pitcher of Sangria and settled back in my chair to relax, then opened the door for conversation by asking her about herself. She answered questions ranging from how many siblings she had to what she did for work. I even asked about her experiences so far on our dating site, *Match*. I had an entire repertoire of questions that I had never asked during our prior phone conversations. I was somewhat curious to learn about her.

What I found was that she either didn't like to talk or she just didn't find me charming, attractive or worth her while, maybe all three because her answers were seldom more than one word, "Yes. No. Pretty good. Uneventful." It got to the point that I was ready to give up all effort to pry a conversation out of her, and I frankly didn't want to work so hard on making small talk. "Where's the waiter when you need him?" I thought to myself. It was looking like that would be the only possible diversion from this uncomfortable gathering.

Finally, our food was served. It seemed like hours had passed since we placed our order, and I started chowing down as if I hadn't had a morsel of food for days. With food in my mouth,

Little Italy...Little In Common

the awkward silence between us was a bit less torturous, but I was still eager to finish and bring the date to a quick conclusion.

Just as I was finishing my pasta Marisa looked up at me and said, "I read an interesting article in a magazine recently about the top sexual fantasies of women."

I almost choked on my linguini, but eked out, "Excuse me?"

"Yes," she said. "There was a great article about what women fantasize most about in the bedroom. Would you like to hear them?"

I think I had stopped sucking in a linguini noodle and left it hanging from my mouth as she took me by surprise starting this conversation. She was actually speaking in sentences AND (in capital letters) she was talking about something sexual. She went on to say that the first fantasy was girl-on-girl. She said women fantasize all the time about being with another woman in the bedroom, and especially being seduced by a girl unexpectedly. Second on the list was sex with a stranger, a stranger defined as someone you don't know and someone who doesn't know you and someone you will never again see. Marisa was on a roll and all of a sudden I decided this little get-together just went from the worst date I ever had to one of my best.

"Number 3. Submission - being tied down and at the mercy of your partner. Four. Sex in Public – either being watched by someone who is hidden or being in front of a big picture window where onlookers are watching. Five. Six. Seven. Eight. Nine and Ten, Sex with Multiple Men at Same Time – i.e. gangbang."

When she said the word "gangbang" that's when my dangling linguini noodle actually fell onto my lap. This girl, who said nothing throughout the whole meal, suddenly had me turned on like I've never been before! I don't know if it was from the "dirty" conversation, me imagining the acts she described or just my adrenaline from this shocking turn of events. Whatever the reason, I was suddenly in love!

Then I asked her if she had fulfilled those fantasies for herself and she admitted she had, except for a couple of them. I had no reservation now about asking her for a second date and, trust me, I began anticipating how soon it could be scheduled.

Marisa and I dated for several months, and although I won't disclose the two fantasies she never tried prior to meeting me, I will say that all her fantasies had been met during our relationship.

Take-Away: Not all conversations go smoothly in the beginning. Some take time to develop. Although you might think the person isn't "into you", stick it out. You never know what may trigger a swing in the other direction.

Menu Flambé

I was going on a date with a girl I met from New York. This was my first online experience and I was a little nervous about meeting for the first time. But to my delight, she looked just like her photo. She was strikingly beautiful with an amazing figure.

The restaurant we met at was a famous steak house known for its sophisticated and romantic dining. The place was decorated with heavy tapestries and had low lighting, which created a relaxing ambiance. There were lit candles on each table and fresh cut flowers arranged with perfection throughout the place. Soft music played in the background.

We were seated and I started our evening with a champagne toast. Being the classy guy that I am, I took every measure to assure my lady's comfort. She was gracious and delightful. We found that we had a lot in common as we chatted over an appetizer.

After about half an hour, we were ready to order our meal. I summoned the waiter to bring the menu. As we were reading the narrative entrée descriptions in it, I didn't realize I was holding mine over the lit candle on the table. It caught fire. It happened so unexpectedly that on instinct I just dropped the thing on the table, which then set the table ablaze.

Someone screamed, "Fire!"

Luckily the maître d instantly took action and grabbed a fire extinguisher, quickly smothering the blaze with white foamy stuff that was propelled all over our table. You can imagine the alarming ruckus that occurred during those moments. But when things calmed back down and no one had been harmed in any way, our entire romantic table setting was destroyed.

The irony of the whole evening was that Lisa and I had a great story to tell our friends about our first date. We ended up seeing each other for nearly a year after that.

My Bloody Valentine

Can you imagine my surprise when I got contacted by a drop dead gorgeous girl from Beverly Hills, California? I live in Florida, some two thousand miles away, and although I'm considered to be a reasonably good looking guy, I was at a loss as to why she would be interested in me. Why would a former beauty pageant queen be interested in a non-famous, not wealthy guy like me? Could it be that it was a mistake? Maybe someone was playing a joke on me? I responded anyway.

I learned that my goddess's name was Lauren. She explained that she was going to be traveling to my neck of the woods in about a month and thought it would be fun to meet someone new out of her area. She said she'd been online for almost a year and hadn't found anyone she really clicked with, so looking in a totally new territory seemed like a good idea. Whatever her reasons for contacting me, I didn't care.

I had her number now and had every intention of moving this beauty queen connection to an actual, live and in-person date as soon as possible. We agreed on a plan to meet in Florida the following month.

Our phone conversations continued over the following two weeks and she proved herself to be smart, sexual and sincere. I was sold on her, sight unseen at this point, and convinced that

I couldn't wait any longer to meet her. So with Valentine's Day just around the corner, I decided to move things along a little quicker. I asked her if she'd be interested in being my Valentine and let me take her to dinner in Beverly Hills on the traditional night of romance. She accepted. She told me the name of her favorite restaurant and we agreed to meet in lobby there the following Saturday evening. I wasn't going to let a couple thousand miles stop me from finding true romance.

The next day I made reservations at The Palms Restaurant and booked a seat for my air travel as well. I called a dog sitter to schedule keeping my pooch, and then made hotel reservations. Since this would be our first date, I felt like I needed my own place to stay so I booked a nice suite at a Beverly Hills hotel. Prices there were expensive, but since I was flying all the way across country to take Lauren to dinner, now was no time to start skimping. I didn't want this goddess to ever think I was cheap. Besides, I didn't know whether I'd get a second chance with this beauty queen so the first date had to make an impression.

My flight to LA was leaving early Saturday afternoon and with the three hour time difference, I knew I'd have plenty of time to check into my hotel, get dressed and meet Lauren at the restaurant as agreed. I had dined at The Palms before, so that took some of the logistical unknowns out of the equation for me. I was confident our meal would be excellent, and I intended to be at my dapper best. As I was preparing to leave home for the Palm Beach Airport, I set my baggage at the front door and made a double check on my to-do list. Lastly was to put my dog in his room with his food, bed and toys as the dog sitter would not be coming until later in the afternoon. I gave him a special treat, a dried pig's ear, as sort of a peace offering to relieve my guilt for leaving him with a sitter, and he was a dog who would make you feel that way. When I went to pet him on the head to say goodbye, he suddenly snapped and bit my hand. He had never bitten me before. Maybe he thought I was going to take his pig's ear away, but whatever the reason I was taken totally by surprise that my devoted dog would do this. I was absolutely shocked and then saw blood streaming down my arm.

I quickly wrapped a towel around my wrist and hand. I didn't know what to do because the towel was turning red from my bleeding hand. I wasn't sure how badly I was injured and knew if I went to the hospital, I'd miss my flight. Do I cancel my hotel reservations, which would cost me $400? Do I cancel my flight, which would cost me $500? My head swirled over how much this trip would cost me if I didn't go, not to mention the fact that I would totally screw up Lauren's Valentine's Day. My head was in a swirl as I watched the towel get even more soaked with blood. The clock was ticking and a decision had to be made quickly.

I chose to make the trip. I put a new towel over my hand and it seemed that the bleeding had subsided. I was in some pain, but hustling now to make my flight was preoccupying my attention. I made a quick stop at Walgreen's and bought several packages of gauze, tape and a big bottle of peroxide. When I got to the airport, I parked in the garage and did a self-medical procedure. I doused my puncture wounds with the peroxide and wrapped my entire hand with the gauze. There was still a small amount of blood soaking through, but I didn't have time to worry about it. I dashed into the airport and used the self check-in kiosk, then proceeded to security. That's when it dawned on me that I could have some trouble ahead. The TSA most certainly would be looking at my bloody, bandaged hand with suspicion. I started getting very nervous that they might not even let me on my flight.

TSA did pull me aside. I get that, someone with a bloodied hand should raise a flag, but thank goodness they didn't detain me very long and I made my flight after going through secondary screening and x-raying and a few more prying questions. California, here I come! I will admit it was embarrassing being stared at on the plane. I looked like a one-armed, bloody bandit. Even the lady at the car rental booth in LA gave me a fifth degree interrogation and never stopped eyeing me suspiciously, but she gave me a car and I arrived at my hotel, checked in and headed straight for the shower. I put clean bandaging on my dog-bitten hand and dressed for dinner.

When I got to the restaurant, I spotted Lauren right away. She was beautiful, more beautiful than her pictures. She immediately asked about my bandaged hand and I gave her the short version of what had happened. She wanted to take me to ER right then, insisting that was more important than dinner. To compromise I promised I would go to have it checked immediately after our meal. She reluctantly agreed, and we sat down for a wonderful meal together. It didn't even seem like a first date. It was warm and comfortable, and who would have imagined I would get so much mileage out of my bit hand? She was flattered beyond belief that I flew across country so selflessly, bleeding the whole way, just to be there for her. Obviously, I didn't ruin the flow by making mention of the nonrefundable hotel and airline costs I'd have been stuck with had I cancelled at the last minute. There was no need to ruin her impression of my gallantry and heroic quest, right?

As promised, we went to Mt. Sinai Hospital after dinner. I got a couple of shots and a butterfly bandage to keep the scarring minimal. I guess I could have used stitches, but since I had waited so long for treatment they didn't feel it was necessary. They professionally wrapped my hand and I was released to go.

Lauren ended up staying with me at my hotel where she confided in me that she loved hotel sex, and although this was only our first date, I didn't put up a fight. After all, it was Valentine's Day. We toasted each other with champagne and Lauren chimed in, "To my new sweetheart, my new love of my life, and my bloody Valentine!"

Lauren and I dated for about a year. It was a great relationship, but the distance between Florida and California was ultimately the deal breaker for us. I'm glad she was a part of my life and thank you, *Match.com*, for bringing this goddess to me. I would have never met her without you!

I Think I Killed Your Dog

I met a great girl on *Match.com* years ago. We both loved the adventure of discovering new restaurants and travelling, but more significant was the fact that we shared a passion for rescue dogs.

Marci and I had been dating a couple of weeks when she told me she had to go out of town on business. Since she had just moved to New York City a month earlier and hadn't yet established much of a new circle of friends, I was the obvious pick to be her little Shih Tzu's dog sitter while she was away. I thought the timing was really good for me because I had just recently lost my Lab to old age and missed the company of a dog around the house.

So Marci stopped at my place the night before her trip and gave me a list of nearly a hundred things I was to do in caring for little Maddie. She had typed out a schedule that showed what times and how much to feed Maddie morning, noon and night as well as when to walk her. There was also a typed narrative of her favorite doggie games and how to play them with her. She made suggestions for other pooch activities, where to put her bed and how it should be fluffed each day. Do you think Marci could be classified as a micro-manager or just an over-protective doggie-mother? Either way, I was happy to have the cute pup for company and assured Marci I would take very good care of her.

That night after putting Maddie to bed exactly as instructed, I awoke suddenly in the middle of the night. I thought I should check on Maddie and when I looked in on her, she was lying on her side and appeared to be sleeping. However, when I looked closer I could tell she was breathing heavily. Something was wrong. Something was terribly wrong.

Next to Maddie's bed was my television cabinet and I immediately noticed the lower door open. There were pellets scattered on the floor in front of it, and in a nanosecond I realized to my horror what must have happened. My pest control people had placed a rodent trap inside that cabinet just a week earlier and Maddie must have chewed into the cardboard container.

Of course Marci had left her vet's phone number but it was two o'clock in the morning. I was terrified that Maddie had been poisoned and knew I couldn't wait until normal office hours to get medical intervention, so I called the vet's number. I got an answering service and they said the doctor would call me back. I waited. I was beginning to panic as I imagined the terrible fate the little dog might be facing if I didn't get help soon. The sound of my voice on the phone caused Maddie to open her eyes. She sat up.

I was distraught. Maddie sat quietly, just watching me. I was scared what might happen. Then my phone rang and I grabbed it, "Hello! Hello!"

My heart was pounding as I poured out the story of the rodent poison and the pellets on the floor and the heavy breathing. When I took a breath, the vet literally commanded me to calm down and said, "get the container the dog chewed into and read to me the warning on it."

I can't express my relief when he told me not to worry. The pellets in the trap turned out not to be poisonous, but he said ingesting them would cause the dog to feel nausea and have a loss of appetite for a few days. He instructed me to give her some Pepto-Bismol and she would be just fine for the night.

Luckily I had some PB tablets in my medicine cabinet and gave her one in some cheese, which she gulped right down. Obviously the loss of appetite had not kicked in yet. The vet then said I could pick up some pills from his office the next morning that would take care of any further symptoms she might have from having eaten the rodent pellets.

I ended up sleeping with Maddie in my office that night and in the morning she seemed to be perfectly fine. Did I escape the bullet or what?

When Marcie called to check in that afternoon she of course asked how her beloved little Maddie was doing. I gave a positively raving report. I told her Maddie was happy and I couldn't be enjoying her company more. I decided to never spill the beans on what could have been Maddie's painful scrape with death at the hands of ME, her trusted and highly IRRESPONSIBLE dog sitter! Imagine if I had to tell my new girlfriend, "Sweetheart, I have bad news. I killed your dog." I doubt the relationship would have lasted past the phone call, but all's well that ends well. Marcie and I were together for almost ten years. I take that back…Marcie, Maddie and I were together for almost ten years.

Drive By

Charly has found a new dating website called *MissTravel.com*. It's different than most dating sites because there are only three meeting options allowed for a first date. You can offer your selected partner an all-expense paid trip to your own hometown, their hometown or a neutral city. Whoever makes the invitation pays for the date. Reports are that there have been some pretty extravagant trips arranged to Europe, Asia and even one to Australia. The typical member on the site is a financially successful guy who is offering a trip to a hot, beautiful woman, but women are not excluded from extending invitations too.

Charly became a regular on the site and liked to fly girls into his hometown, Chicago. He had had a couple of bad experiences though with girls who ended up not looking like their pictures. More often than not when this happened, they either looked much younger in their photos or much thinner. He never knew for sure just what he was getting until he actually picked his date up at the airport. What he hoped for every time was proving to be a hit or miss endeavor. Since he was pretty particular about his women, a miss instead of a hit would ruin his whole weekend.

By his sixth planned trip through the site, he decided on a foolproof system to avoid any more disappointing weekend forays. He planned that he would tell his date to look for his red Porsche Carrera convertible at the airport pickup curb and that's where they'd meet after her flight arrived in Chicago. However, what he didn't tell was that he was actually driving a blue BMW. That way he could show up at curbside incognito and see what the girl looked like. If she looked like her photo, he would introduce himself, tell her he brought his other car and the two would drive off for a fun-filled weekend. If the girl didn't look like her photo, well…shame on her. He figured if she could misrepresent herself to him, he would misrepresent himself to her and drive away without her ever knowing he had been there. Yes, the gal would be left cold at curbside, consequentially resulting in both MIA for the weekend. .. no explanations ever told.

Take-Away: Ladies, there are a lot of creeps out there. Let the guy come to you first. If he has good intentions, he'll go out of his way for you. If he's not willing to in the beginning, he never will.

Identity Theft

Talk about mistaken identity. I met a girl on a dating site and we arranged to meet at a popular bar and restaurant after work one evening. As I had been on the site for several weeks already, I was becoming overwhelmed in trying to keep track of my dates, their profiles, pictures and especially all the girls' names. As I was driving to the restaurant to meet this date, I realized I couldn't remember her name. *Was this one Kathy or was Kathy my date tomorrow night? No. No. Jennifer is tonight and Casey is tomorrow.*

I was genuinely confused and realized I was going to have to use my magic faking act when I arrived because I didn't even know what this girl looked like. I was hoping the bar wouldn't be crowded so it would be easier for both of us to spot each other. Of course it turned out that the place was jam packed.

I parked my car and hoped I was slick enough to pull this off. I pushed my way in the door of the bar. It was noisy and loud, and to make matters even more chaotic, there was a guy playing the piano accompanied by a bongo player, of all things! The good thing though was that there was a large, u-shaped bar in the place so I at least had a defined pathway to follow as I befuddled my way along through the crowd. Finally I caught eyes with a gal who motioned me in her direction. I was relieved because I figured she recognized me from my profile. We shook hands, but the noise was so loud I wasn't quite sure if she addressed me by my name. I pointed toward the restaurant and she followed.

The restaurant was somewhat quieter. We had a nice but short dinner together because it was still a strain to carry on a conversation due to the noise from the bar area. In spite of that, it was a good date and I knew we had some chemistry going between us. My magic fake act succeeded in me getting her name without her realizing I didn't know it, Jennifer. So from my viewpoint, that was a good starting point because I was definitely interested in seeing her again.

However, a bad thing happened when I walked her out the door at the end of our meal. She said, "It was a pleasure meeting you, Bob." I smiled and gave her a kiss on the cheek not knowing if I should tell her my name was actually Tom, not Bob. I said nothing about it. I simply told her I'd love to see her again and she said, "Ditto."

When I got back home that evening I went to check my emails on the dating site and saw a message that read, "Thanks a lot, asshole." It turned out it was from Meghan, the girl I was supposed to meet. She thought I had stood her up. And now it made sense why Jennifer called me Bob. Jennifer was supposed to meet a guy named Bob, and I was supposed to meet this girl named Meghan. What a mix up!

At any rate, I started dating Jennifer and it wasn't until we were dating exclusively that I told her my name wasn't Bob. I explained the mix up and she was embarrassed as heck that she'd been calling me by the wrong name for weeks. She asked why I hadn't told her sooner and I confessed I was afraid she'd be mad. I told her I thought she would think I had gone along with the mistaken identity to keep her from seeking out the real Bob, and since I liked her so much I didn't want to take the risk of maybe losing her. She thought that was sweet, and we were together for almost a year.

Kelly Girl

I'm signed up on *Match.com* and recently encountered a situation that put me in a dilemma. I've been trying to figure out how to handle it.

I met a great girl named Kelly. She is a very attractive tall blond with blue eyes. She's sexy as heck and more than graciously endowed with a jaw-dropping feminine physique that most guys can only dream about, if you know what I mean. I can't believe she hasn't been a cover girl for my favorite magazine, "Maxim". How I was so lucky to find her on such a popular dating site is beyond me, but I did and we have been dating for several weeks now. There is no question she likes me.

I recently invited her for a weekend trip and she accepted. Now although we've fooled around together, we haven't had sex yet so it's a no-brainer to imagine that consummating our relationship over the weekend would be on my radar screen, right? Right, and it was obviously on hers as well, which is why she dropped the bomb shell on me a couple of days ago that put me in this confusing dilemma.

She explained to me that she is a hermaphrodite. She said she was genetically born a boy, but she is really a girl. I was confused. She went on to say that she displays all the female characteristics and is female in every way on the outside, but on the inside has male parts. I was still confused. She said she's not a transsexual in the sense of being born a man and believing she's a girl due to no male chromosomes, or maybe she said she was missing a female chromosome, I can't remember. My head was spinning. I could tell she was trying to measure my surprise and concerns, and then tried to put it in perspective by referring to Jamie Lee Curtis who was likewise born a hermaphrodite.

"Look how well she turned out and how much she is respected as a beautiful actress."

I nodded my head to agree, but had so much going on in my brain at that point I wasn't at all convinced that Jamie Lee's beauty and success had anything to do with Kelly and me at the moment. Somehow it just didn't seem the same. Jamie Lee's was a Hollywood story that I read about once; this was real, up front and personal. That made it different.

I like Kelly a lot, but I don't know that I'm mentally mature enough to continue dating her. The fact that she still has male genitalia but has every part of a woman on the outside is what's got me confused. It's like an oxymoron, a little hard to understand. If she hadn't ever told me about her unusual circumstance, I would have never guessed it in a million years, but I'm glad she did since I suppose I would have discovered it soon enough. So I told her I needed to take some time to sort the whole thing out. She seemed to completely understand. No doubt she had been through the discussion with other guys in the past and was prepared for whatever reaction came.

At this point I'm leaning in the direction that I won't continue dating her. As great as she is, I just don't think I can handle it. I have no doubt she will find someone who can and they will both be lucky to have found each other.

I think I'm going to miss her a lot.

A Real Conundrum

I was at a loss for words after getting a wink from someone on one of the popular online dating sites that I frequent. It was sent from a very pretty Asian girl. I was flattered. For me, getting winks from beautiful women make my day because I am normally one of those shy-type guys who get a little nervous when beauties pay me attention. I have a hard time taking compliments, and so I always have to muster my courage to respond.

Upon reading the profile of my latest admirer, I was a little taken back. She wrote: "I'm an Asian pre-op transsexual. A girl who functions and lives as a woman for ten years now. I'm sexy, smooth, long black hair pre-op with 36-26-36 body. I'm prettier than most women for sure. I'm a hostess in a popular restaurant and nobody suspects I'm not a woman. I love to look pretty at all times, spa, facials, manis and pedis. I love fashion, and looking to enjoy and have the greatest things in life."

I'm scaring myself now because I never imagined I would ever consider responding to someone like this. I've always thought of myself as a full hetero male, a guy who has had multiple long term committed relationships with women. The thought of me dating a guy has always been a repulsive notion.

However, this girl was beautiful, sincere and smart. She had all the qualities of a woman I was looking for, except one. She wasn't a woman.

I decided to meet her for drinks anyway. I thought it would make a great story at my next cocktail party. We met one evening and believe it or not, she was not only as beautiful as her pictures, but couldn't have been more sweet and warm. If she had never told me she wasn't a real woman, I would have never known. Our conversation that night was engaging and delightful. I kept hoping I wouldn't feel any physical attraction toward her, but I did, and all that we had in common made our connection even more appealing. So when it was time to bring our first date to an end, I told her I would call her again.

Now I'm sitting in a conundrum. I'm conflicted. I have called her since that first date and we are continuing to keep in touch, but my rational mind keeps getting in the way of my attraction to her. I'm imagining a platonic friendship would be okay, but I'm just not sure at this point that would work. Only time will tell, and I'll keep you posted on where we go from here.

The $5,000 Perfect Girlfriend

My quest to find the perfect girlfriend has been challenging, to say the least. So I decided to try a new dating site, one that is for singles seeking travel companions. Since other dating sites had failed to take me to my treasure, I abandoned those old "ships" and boarded this travel site with renewed hope and determination. I put on my pirate hat and likened myself to Johnny Depp, imagining a high seas adventure while cruising

The $5,000 Perfect Girlfriend

Royal Caribbean. "Ar-r-r-gh," I haughtily say to myself. "Sail me into the sunset under the magical spell of balmy skies, tis the perfect way to capture that chest of gold, the perfect girlfriend."

I studied the women's bios the way any good pirate would examine a treasure map, and I made a date with a girl. We met at a popular restaurant in Boca Raton, Florida on a warm Saturday evening. She was beautiful! Everything about her appearance was amazing and I thought more than once she could have rivaled the best of any playboy bunny centerfold.

We talked for a while about one topic then the next, and found that we shared in common favorite foods, vacation spots and activities. I was really getting the feeling that she liked me and the chemistry between us was good. Kim then asked what I was looking for from the travel site and I told her that I wanted a traveling companion who had the ability to laugh with me, have great conversations and someone I could introduce to family, friends and clients. I told her the woman would have to be a person who was a classy dresser, from black tie to casual chic, and most importantly someone I could have a great intimate relationship with. (Yes, I was talking sex!)

She looked me straight in the face and asked, "What are you willing to pay for all those attributes?" "Excuse me," I asked.

Then she said, "I would think if you could find a woman who could provide you with all of that, who could relieve you of all your stresses and pressures, it would be priceless, right?"

Now she had my imagination running rampant. As a matter of fact, my mind was so caught up in itself, my tongue was tied and all this bumbling pirate could utter was, "I guess so."

She then went on to make a very straight-forward proposal. She said, "Just pay me $5,000 a month and I will be your perfect girlfriend. I will do whatever you want and I won't ever disagree or argue with you. You will think you've died and gone to heaven!"

I felt a warm and cunning smile come over my face. *Is she serious?* I had never expected anything like this from a date, much less a first date, but in a strange way the idea was enticing and made sense to me. She went on to explain that we could sign a contract, not a marriage contract, but a personal consulting contract. The contract would be good for ninety days and renewed thereafter by mutual consent. *This is insane. No, this is too good to be true!* My mind was spinning and then I heard the voice of wisdom scream louder, "This is crazy!"

But the impetuous pirate in me took control of my mouth and I blurted, "Let's do it!"

She told me she would email me a contract, dating it the first of the upcoming month, which was only five days away. She kissed me sweetly as she got up to leave the table and stroked the back of my neck. My pirate boots felt heavy, as if filled to the brim with water, and I couldn't move. I hardly recall saying goodbye as I sat there watching her gracefully flow out the front door of the restaurant.

Instead of finding treasure, this pirate's imaginative quest just might have gotten him caught like a fish - hook, line and sinker!

"The Good"

A Friend With Benefits

It took a long time but I think that I finally met the girl of my dreams online. She advertised herself as a girl who wasn't looking for a commitment. She said, "at this point in my life, I'm more suitable for a nsa relationship (no strings attached) until I figure out what I want in a life partner. Every relationship experience I've had put me one step closer to figuring that out, because I take lessons, the good and the bad, to learn what I need to do.

When I met Angela, she was even prettier than her pictures, if that is even possible. She was Latina with the best figure I've ever seen on a woman. She explained to me that she's had so many boyfriends, fiancés over the years and she found them all to be controlling. They would buy her gifts, lease her cars, give her credit cards, etc. and by accepting these gifts, she felt owned. These were powerful guys who were used to getting their own way and buying beautiful things, and that's all I was to them… another possession. But what they didn't realize she explained to me was that "once I was over them and didn't enjoy being with them anymore, and didn't see myself with them for the rest of my life, I would leave them. Give them back everything they gave me, and just walk out. I'm not in it for the money. I just want to be happy, and once the experience isn't fun any longer, I'm out of there."

"So what exactly are you looking for," I asked. " I don't think I'm asking too much," Angela said. "I want good times, new experiences, laughter and great kinky sex." She said that she's always been attracted to older and powerful men, but she hates being patronized. "It's my biggest turnoff," Angela said, "especially when I feel it's done by someone who is not as smart or as sharp as me. So, I'm really simple to figure out. Just be smarter and sharper than me, or at least on my level, and we'll get along great. One more thing, whenever I summon you for sex, no matter what time of the day or night, you better be here within 30 minutes or I will no longer have any more use for you. Is that clear?"

It sure was clear. Not only do I still see Angela regularly, and enjoying my goddess that has been sent to me from above, but for the first time in my life, I am never late for an appointment anymore. In fact, with Angela, I'm actually early every time. Pavlov had nothing on me.

Too Good To Be True!

Despite the fact that I went to a top university, I'm questioning my own intelligence. Maybe I'm just naïve. I'm not sure.

I recently went on a dating website that I learned about while watching *20/20* on television. The site specializes in people who want to meet through travel. Since I love spending weekends in Las Vegas to discharge my stress, I thought that inviting a young lady to join me there would be fun, relaxing and different. I had no idea what different would mean until I came across my date's profile.

It read: *I'm a fun good person. Very untraditional kind of girl. Looking for an open minded person. I'm the best of both worlds. If you love a sexy girl on your arm or a cute drinking buddy to go out with, hit me up. If you're someone who loves mixing things up in life, creative and love change, hit me up.*

She sounded perfect for me and we began texting back and forth for several weeks prior to meeting. She's a professional model and sent me several pictures of herself. Some of them were bathing suit shots and some were photos of her in formal dress and casual wear. She was stunningly beautiful, and I was really looking forward to meeting this open minded, untraditional girl. Her name was Angelina.

I booked a suite at the Venetian Hotel in Vegas and made arrangements for Angelina to meet me there. Her flight from Phoenix was a redeye special, and she arrived knocking at my hotel suite door just after midnight. When I unfastened the latch to greet her and finally got to lay my eyes on my weekend date, she looked like a goddess. She was better than her pictures and came dressed in a short skirt, thigh-high boots and a low cut, skin tight halter top. She was a knock-out!

We decided to go down to the casino, have a few drinks and get to know each other better. After four hours in the bar and way too many drinks, we went back up to my room where we both found ourselves exhausted. We went right to sleep without even fooling around despite the fact that she had slipped into an invitingly sexy little nightie. We agreed that getting to know each other under the blankets would have to wait until morning.

Well, Angelina and I did get to know each other that way the following morning, but it wasn't a morning frolic in the bed, it was a nooner-til-three. It just so happened that it was her "time of the month" and in spite of that issue, I'm just going to say she satisfied me like no other woman had in quite a long time! We headed down to the pool where we spent the rest of the afternoon and enjoyed a poolside lunch and cocktails. Angelina wore a bikini that was the most spectacular bathing suit I've ever seen. Everyone around the pool stared when she breast stroked her away across the water. I felt like I was a lucky guy to be in her presence.

That evening we had an amazing dinner at an Italian restaurant in the hotel and then to see Celine Dion's show at Caesar's Palace. The show was great and again I felt proud to have Angelina on my arm. She wore a spectacular and very revealing gown that was another attention-getter.

We went back to the hotel afterward and I did some gambling. Angelina hung out next to me and brought me luck. We continued having cocktails until two in the morning when we finally returned to the room. We fell right to sleep like two people who had known each other for years and comfortable knowing the love-making would come in the morning. It did and again Angelina was a real pleaser. Her intimacy skills were beyond my expectations. By noon that day I felt a little bad that I wasn't able to reciprocate, but she happily smiled and said, "Next trip it will be all about me."

We hung out all afternoon at the pool again, and Angelina didn't disappoint with that day's bathing suit selection. It was a black, stop-you-in-your-tracks one-piece. By late in the afternoon we headed back to the room and I was again left with a big smile on my face. She told me she hoped it would last me until we saw each other again, and with that she dashed off to catch her flight home.

I left Vegas the next day. It was a sensational weekend and I must say that Angelina has captured my attention in a special way although I can't totally put my finger on why. She was sexy, funny and, oh boy does she know how to please a man! It was odd though in a way that she was not interested in letting me explore her body much at all. I'm not a selfish guy in the bed and truly wanted to pleasure her in some way, but I guess I'll have to wait until our next date to get the opportunity. There's something about that girl that's different from the rest and next time we're together I will figure it out. Do you think she could be a …….? No, couldn't be.

Naughty But Nice

Okay, I'm not naïve. I've been on several internet dating sites over the years and I don't mean kinky ones either. *Match.com* and *MissTravel.com* are considered decent and respectable in the world of internet dating sites, right? And I realize too that although no individual site ever mentions the word sex or sexual relations in exchange for money, any inferences to that sort of thing must be negotiated offsite/offline or simply left to one's own imagination.

With that said, I answered a profile recently with the caption "Naughty but Nice". It also contained a byline which read "Classy with a Naughty Side". There was nothing sexual implied in the profile and the pictures of the young lady were both casual and elegant. In fact, she described herself as "…a sweet and natural girl who enjoys many things life has to offer. I love to travel and spend time in the company of a gentleman who has much to teach me and share about life, places and experiences."

Now THAT sounded like my kind of a woman!

So, I wrote to my potential date and told her a little about myself. I explained that I was looking for a fun type of girl who loved to travel and play, one who hopefully had little baggage (meaning no responsibilities) and knew how to treat her man in exchange for a great and happy relationship together. I was sincere in describing what I was seeking. From my viewpoint, what I wrote was straight forward, plain and simple. I could hardly wait to set a date with this gal.

The reply I got back from her read exactly as follows:

I'm definitely the perfect match for you. I'm dirty, a submissive little slut and loads of fun. I also give the best BJ's in the world.

I couldn't believe it. It took me totally by surprise. I reread my initial message to her several times to see whether I might have inadvertently encouraged that kind of answer; I certainly didn't intend to. Maybe my language about knowing how to "treat her man" was misconstrued as some sexual overture. I swear I never intended to sound like I was on the prowl, but she obviously took it that way. Now I have a dilemma on my mind. Should I write her back? What should I say? Do I dare meet her for a drink?

So many questions, so little time. What's a guy to do? Hmmm… not sure, but I'm thinking she could be my next wife!

The Office Perk

I just joined a new real estate office and as I was getting familiar with my new environment, an agent came in and walked straight through the front office toward her desk. I heard two senior brokers in back of me saying, "Oh, my God! Here comes my goddess of love."

Sounded pretty chauvinistic to me and probably in any other professional office would have been grounds for a sexual harassment suit, but something told me that these guys weren't going to take disciplinary mandates for their behavior from anyone. The agent ignored them. I uttered not a peep, but couldn't help eyeballing her as she sashayed past my desk. In my head, I heard myself repeating their words as she disappeared down the hallway. Her name was Jennifer.

When she walked into the office she was really a sight for sore eyes. She wore a short skirt, low cut blouse and high heels. She was a vision. I'm not necessarily sure that was appropriate attire for an agent, but who was I to complain. When Paul and Arnie made such a commotion over her, it actually kind of turned me off. Believe me, I appreciate beauty more than any guy but I've also found that a woman who is constantly receiving attention for her looks is the type of woman I do not do well with. It's not that I'm insecure because I am a fairly good looking guy, but I tend to be a little shy around beautiful women. I usually don't approach a girl if she's all full of herself because that's when my insecurity kicks in, and Jennifer definitely gave off that vibe. I surmised pretty quickly that she no doubt had multiple boyfriends and the bottom line was that she was out of my league. I didn't give any of it another thought.

About three weeks after joining this new real estate company, I signed up for *Match.com*. I had been on it in the past, but never really met anyone that I was interested in. But now that I had moved to a new home and area, I felt inspired to start going out and meeting new people. So after putting my profile and pictures up, I started my online search for dating prospects.

To my surprise, the next day I got a reply from a girl whose user name was "Sexy Lexy." I opened the message. It said, "Hello handsome. I think you work in my office and after reading your profile, I think we have so much in common. Hope you read mine and agree. I have not posted a picture as I don't want others to know my personal business, but if you send me your email address, I'd be happy to privately send you some. Hopefully I'll look familiar to you and you'll want to pursue. Anxious to hear from you."

It was signed Sexy Lexy.

I was very curious to know who in the office was writing to me, and I didn't remember anyone by the name of Lexy. I promptly sent her back a reply with my email address.

The next day I heard back from Lexy. I could hardly believe that it was Jennifer from my office. The girl who I thought was totally unapproachable was actually pursuing me. Who would have thought? The pictures she sent were very sexy poses. They showed her in shorty shorts, mini-skirts and a couple of bikini shots as well. She looked gorgeous and I found myself anxious to pursue her diligently.

We made a date for dinner the following weekend and she recommended that I pick her up at her house. She suggested that we have a drink there first and then go to dinner. She asked me to come at 8:00 p.m. and dress casually as she wanted to go to a certain waterfront café near her home. I could hardly wait to see her again because she hadn't been into the office once since that first day. Paul had told me that she rarely came into the office, and because he was one of the catcallers when I first saw Jennifer, I didn't tell him that I had a date with her. There was really no need to rub it in his face and make myself look better than him. And besides, I had no idea how the date would go. For all I knew, she might not even be interested in me after our first date.

I got to Jennifer's house and after ringing the bell, I heard steps in the background. When the door opened up, there was Jennifer standing in the doorway dressed in the sexiest lingerie I have ever seen. I must have looked like the deer in the headlights staring at her. I was totally taken by her beauty and in shock that she was dressed that way. I had no complaints, but was at a complete loss for words. Finally, I uttered, "Am I early? Do you need more time to get ready?"

She slowly smiled and said, "I am ready. Are you?"

With that she took my hand and led me inside. She asked what I wanted to drink and I knew I needed something strong to shock myself back to reality. I kept thinking that my office buddies were never going to believe this. I didn't even believe it!

Needless to say, Jennifer and I never made it to dinner that night. In fact, we spent all weekend locked inside her house. It was my best and longest dinner date ever. We dated for about 6 months and we're the best of friends. Even though we work in the same office, it took *Match.com* to make the connection for us. I count my blessings every day, and although I don't know for certain how long this dream will last, I do know that I love my benefits at work!

Money Can Buy Happiness

You've heard the theory that money can't buy happiness. And I've been brought up with the belief that if you don't have your health, it doesn't matter how much money you have. I'm still a believer in both, but I must say, thanks to the online dating sites available today you can literally buy all the love and happiness you could ever want! Well, maybe more accurately would be to say you can buy all the lust you could ever want.

I answered an ad recently on an online dating site that specializes in women looking to go on vacations with men and vice versa. The site caught my interest with its slogan "You have the money to travel but you don't like traveling alone. Find beautiful singles, travel girls and travel companions to join you."

I studied the website profiles searching for a companion to join me on a weekend getaway to St.Barts, and found one who looked like the perfect woman for me. She was a gal who said she loved to have fun and be wild. She said she wanted to be spoiled and taken care of, like any woman does, but in return she claimed she knew how to spoil a man like no other woman. One weekend with her, she said, and you will want to keep coming back for more and more. She promised a weekend that you wouldn't soon forget. Additionally, she made her invitation open to either men or women. Yes, I thought she sounded like the woman of my dreams, and maybe my fantasies too.

The gal called herself Tiffany. I suspected it probably wasn't her real name, but who cares. And even though Tiffany's profile had me convinced she was my girl, there was one more detail in her profile that sealed the deal for certain in my thinking. Reading that one detail made me decide I didn't care how much the weekend trip would end up costing me. Money would be no object. You see Tiffany was an adult film star.

Now I've been on dating sites for years and most women that I meet online are looking for love, companionship and, yes, the "C" word, commitment. But on this particular travel site together with my particular interest in a St Barts getaway, I felt like I had hit the lottery of lust, I mean love, when I found Tiffany's profile.

I sent Tiffany a ticket (turned out that Tiffany was not her real name after all), a gift card to cover travel expenses and we met at one of my favorite resorts. We came face to face for the first time in the lobby on a Saturday morning. She was a beauty. You would have never known she was in the business of porn by looking at her. She was youthful, sweet and innocent. We spent the entire weekend getting to know each other, swimming, laughing, eating and having the time of our lives. I had rented a villa and so it was just like spending the weekend at home with the most exciting, sensual and down to earth woman I've ever met.

But our trip came to an end way too quickly. I couldn't seem to get enough of her and absolutely loved being with her. I didn't want it to be over yet. She felt the same way, so we made arrangements for another trip the following month, same place, same villa, same fun. We both wanted everything the same because nothing else could possibly have been better than what we had experienced. And listen, for a guy who never wanted to commit again, I was ready to marry this girl by the end of our weekend together. I thought she was everything I had ever wanted in a woman and a lot more, but in retrospect I realize I probably wasn't thinking clearly at that point. I didn't propose and most likely never will so long as I keep my head from fogging up.

And if it weren't for websites like this I would have never found this amazing girl. I'm so grateful to whoever first came up with the travel dating concept. It offered me exactly what I was looking for and Tiffany's promise of a weekend that I wouldn't soon forget couldn't have been more on the money.

Take-Away: God bless America!

Buy My Boobs And I'm Yours Forever

I met a very enterprising young lady on a site that specializes in making arrangements. She was blond, blue-eyed and had a great smile. Her profile headline, which is the title of this story, captured my attention. What she wrote in her profile had a tone that was sincere and sweet. I couldn't help but be attracted to it. It read, "All I want is breast implants and I'll be your sugar baby for as long as you'd like me to be. I'd be forever grateful and pleasure you as much as you'd like day and night to show my appreciation and gratitude."

This gal, Jennifer, and I chatted several times on the phone before we met. She lived fairly close to me so it was easy enough to meet for lunch one afternoon. When I asked her what was so important about having bigger breasts she said they would give her more self-confidence around people. She wanted to feel more womanly, and since she couldn't afford to get them on her own, she'd be willing to give herself to a boyfriend if he'd pay for them. She would remain loyal to the guy until he no longer wanted her or until they mutually agreed to split up.

With that she handed me a written contract. It was five pages long. I have no idea where she got it, but I doubt it was drawn up by a licensed attorney because it read more like a master and slave arrangement than a bilateral purchase contract. It committed Jennifer for a minimum of one year. She would perform as a submissive servant. It outlined what her duties would be, from housework to cooking. It even made provisions for how she would dress both inside and out of her master's dwelling, and she had already handwritten my name on the blank line as the master. The contract was detailed and covered every scenario in life you can imagine, including what would happened in the bedroom. In that section, there were some hard limits outlined of things she would never do. There weren't very many items on the forbidden list, but the ones that were there were graphically spelled out.

I was amazed at the amount of time and effort that someone went to in creating a document like this, and I wondered whether it was even legal. It certainly looked and sounded very legalese. I was at a loss for words after reading it and then Jennifer asked me what I thought. I folded it and stuffed it in my pocket, telling her I'd look it over and get back to her later in the week after I made my decision. She seemed disappointed that I didn't sign on the dotted line then and there, but gave me a minimal smile and agreed. I could tell she was she was determined to make this deal work. I felt like I was getting strong-armed by a used car salesman!

The following day Jennifer called and asked if I was ready to sign. I told her I wasn't sure yet. She then asked if I would go with her to the plastic surgeon the next day for her consultation. I held my ground saying I really wasn't sure whether this was something I was interested in getting involved in, but she pleaded that she just wanted my support at the consultation. I gave in and agreed to meet her there.

When we listened to the surgeon's overview of the procedure I learned a lot. He explained the difference between silicone and saline. He showed pictures of how it would look if the implants were placed higher up, giving the appearance of baseballs, and the variation of sizes and amount of cc's. It was frankly more than I ever wanted to know. Finally, an hour later, Jennifer asked me what I thought. I said I was certainly more educated now but still needed time to consider. We left the doctor's office and she told me she understood and would leave me alone for a couple days to think the whole thing over.

And think I did. I really liked this girl and wanted to help her out, but I wasn't comfortable with the idea that signing a contract binding her to serve me was a healthy foundation for a relationship, or even legal for that matter. So I came up with a compromise. I told Jennifer I wanted a relationship with her, starting immediately. No contract, just an easy, stress-free relationship. I told her that if she could keep me happy, and vice versa, and be the perfect girlfriend for six months that I would pay for the breasts she craved.

Her rebuttal was that if I bought them now, then I'd be getting the enjoyment of them.

I insisted that I liked her just the way she was and she was every bit the woman I wanted. I argued that we would be together forever if the first six months worked out and then I'd get to enjoy her bigger breasts for many years. Deal?

With that my Jennifer hugged me and agreed saying, "I'm going to make you the luckiest guy in the world."

She was so grateful that she would be getting her new boobs, and I have no doubt that she'll be my best girlfriend ever.

Three's Company

Talk about hitting the lottery of love! I live in a large home in the Boca Raton area and one Friday night began searching an online dating service that had been strongly recommended to me by a good friend. I looked through some hundred different profiles before I hit the *perfecta* of all ads. It was placed by a lesbian couple who said they were seeking a male Caucasian, age 35 and up, who is both handsome and intelligent. So far so good, I thought.

It read: *He must be able to accommodate us in his home when we're in town, approximately one week a month, and must be down to earth and open minded sexually. We are a sexually uninhibited couple who are fun but not crazy. We love trying new things and just need a place to stay and maybe some transportation. In return, we will rock your world, guaranteed!*

So, I made contact and spoke with Natalie on the phone before setting up a date with her and Eva. In that first conversation, Natalie asked me if I had ever seen the old television show *Three's Company*. I had. Then she told me that she looked a lot like the character Chrissy from the popular sitcom. She described herself as being blonde and extremely busty. She told me that Eva looked a little like the character Janet, brunette and petite. She said the big difference though with them and the show was that the television audience never knew for certain whether or not Jack was "giving it" to his roommates while they lived together. Natalie then said, "You won't have that dilemma if we stay with you. There will be no question at all that you will know everything about us and that we will do whatever you ask…anything at all."

To be honest, at that point in the conversation Natalie had me hooked. I mean, "Hello! This is Dan." Natalie and Eva have been visiting me now for the past several months. We have a very unique and loving relationship, and I am so grateful that I hit my online *perfecta!* Their profile description turned out to be very accurate and I think I'm in love with both of them now. Although I realize not everyone will understand this relationship, all I can say is that for me it has been a match made in heaven.

A Real Trifecta

Just when you think you've seen it all, I maintain that there's always something even more shocking coming on the horizon. What I experienced this past week is a perfect example. I was blown away! I was on a dating site that specialized in vacation dating between single men and women. Although there is no mention of sex anywhere in any description, I think it's implied. Well, just think about it: single men, single women, away from home on a vacation? What's likely to be happening, right?

So I was perusing profiles in that site and came across one that I had never seen listed before. It had a headline that read: *Travel Extravaganza With Three Beautiful Women*. The narrative caption below it said: *Not one, not two, but three. You will always be accompanied by three captivating women with diverse but also similar selections in personalities...how can you go wrong?* Now I can't speak for all my male counterparts, but for me, the chance to spend a vacation with three beautiful ladies sounded like a dream come true. Their profile continued to describe them as being adventurous and willing to accompany their travel date on such activities as rock climbing, sailing, zip lining or you name it. They claimed to be unique ladies who know how to please their man while traveling, exploring and having a good time.

I made contact and suggested a trip for the three day holiday weekend coming up. We agreed we'd all meet up in Vegas and

I made arrangements for their airline tickets from California. While talking to Monica, the spokesperson of the threesome, I explained I would get a suite at the Palazzo for myself and another suite for the three of them. Monica said, "You can do that if you'd like, sweetheart, but why don't you save your money and get just one suite that is big enough for all of us to share? It'll be much cozier that way, don't you agree?" I was at a loss for words.

She then said, "Just make sure it has a king bed, or if they make anything larger than a king, get that." I think my knees started vibrating. My ears got flushed and hot. I began to perspire, but calmly responded by saying I thought her suggestion made complete sense. I wondered if this was just too good to be true and decided I'd have to try my best to keep all expectations in check just in case it turned out to be some disappointing flop.

I'm happy to report that this Vegas weekend was perhaps the best of my life, and that's saying a lot. The ladies didn't disappoint, and it was for lack of a better word....breathtaking. If this was my only online dating experience ever, I would say that I hit the lottery on this one. It really doesn't get any better.

Take-Away: The old theory, "if it sounds too good to be true, then it probably is" doesn't apply in all cases.

Room With A View

I met this gal online and thought she seemed pretty cool. By way of background, you should know that we had talked on the phone at least six or eight times and even exchanged pictures over our 4Gs before we actually got together. I liked her personality and air of self-confidence, but did take note that her pictures were way more explicit than mine. They were quite provocative, but didn't overstep my comfort zone so I continued having phone conversations with her.

When we finally decided to a date, I suggested we meet in the City at one of my favorite places. Somehow she was able to upstage my idea and sell me on a restaurant she liked in the meatpacking area. So that's where I met her on our first get-together. It turned out that her suggestion was a good one, and we both thoroughly enjoyed the cuisine, service and ambiance of the place.

Late into the evening she said she had another good idea. She told me that her favorite hotel was nearby and that she was actually staying there for the weekend. She asked if I wanted to stop over for a nightcap before I went home and I accepted the invite. What guy wouldn't want to follow a beautiful girl back to her hotel?

However, there were two things that made me look pretty naïve that evening. First, I didn't really know that a nightcap wasn't always a drink and, second, the hotel where she was staying was called The Standard, a place I'd never heard of.

Frolicking our way up the street like the two tipsy drunks we were, we stumbled our way into the lobby of The Standard. She hadn't given me the least clue that the place had a rather unique reputation, but I started figuring a few things out very quickly when I saw the non-tinted, floor-to-ceiling windows and luminous inside lighting. Hello? The standard guests who stay at The *Standard* had standards that would not have been standard *at* the Hilton! Believe it or not, the place was perfectly designed for couples who liked to have sex in front of an audience, particularly at night when anyone walking down below on the sidewalk could see every imaginable sort of passion in action, free of charge!

This turned out to be a date with one crazy, uninhibited beautiful girl.

Since that time I've never passed by a hotel without taking a double-glance at the windows. You never know who or what you might see.

*__Take-Away:__ **Hilton or Marriott can learn something from this up and coming hotel concept. This could be the new "Standard" in the hotel industry in the future.**

She Blew My Mind

Recently I signed up on a site called *MissTravel*. I learned about it from the television show *20/20*. The way it works is that usually a guy pays for a gal to fly out to a vacation spot for their first date. The show chronicled a couple who connected on the site and spent their first weekend together in Mexico. Though the couple had never met before, all indications were they had a great time together and their blind date proved to be a success. I thought I'd like to find a woman for the same type of adventure.

So after signing up, I started searching profiles. I found one that impressed me. The girl's name was Paige and I picked her for several reasons. First, she was very pretty, and I related to many details in her profile. Secondly, she lived close to where I live and that was my final deciding factor.

After several telephone conversations and meeting for dinner one evening, we decided to venture away for a vacation together. We agreed on California as our destination because we both loved it there, especially Santa Monica and Malibu. Since she and I were realtors, we knew there'd be plenty of material for conversation to hash over, sharing war stories and so forth. She loved traveling as much as me and what a coincidence that both of us named Italy and Greece as favorite destinations. Top all that common ground with the fact that she also came from the same state as me, Connecticut. Maybe, I thought, this was going to be my perfect woman.

So we met at the airport for our evening flight to California. We were both really excited about going on the trip, but also about getting to know each other better. We took our seats on the plane for the long flight to the West Coast. As an afterthought when making the airline reservations, I decided to upgrade our tickets and this proved to be such a good choice. Our seats were roomy and we had no one sitting on either side of us. Also, there was no one seated in the rows in front of us or behind.

During the first hour of the flight, Paige and I must have consumed ten of those little bottles of vodka. She mixed hers with cranberry juice and I had mine straight up. We talked and talked. Paige giggled and giggled. As the sun was setting in the distant west, the stewardess dimmed the cabin lights. She handed out pillows and blankets for the duration of the flight, and I was thankful because the vodka had definitely caught up with me. I settled back in my chair and drifted off to sleep, super relaxed.

Now this is where my story gets a little risqué. I started having this dream, a sexual dream. I'm sure you've all had one of those dreams that seemed completely real, right? Well, this was a real one! In my dream I was flying first class to somewhere. My seat was more like a Lazyboy recliner than an airplane seat, and I was laid back in it with a blanket over my lap and pillow under my head. It was dark outside and the cabin lighting scant. The sound of the jet's engine was humming like a lullaby. I was so wonderfully comfortable; it was an amazing feeling. There was a woman seated next to me who leaned over my belly and then ducked her head under the blanket on my lap. She began giving me oral sex, and I was in pleasure land!

Well, just as I felt myself nearing a climaxing whammy, I opened my eyes and what I saw startled me. I was confused. Then I realized I hadn't been dreaming at all. Paige's head was under that blanket!

Can you believe that? I had just met this girl on a dating site, and although we had gone out before, we had never had sex. Here she was doing me on an airplane. I couldn't have imagined this in a million years.

Needless to say, our California trip was probably my best vacation in years, and I would have never anticipated finding such a wonderful girl online. I know it may seem like I was crazy about this girl just because she was a sexual animal, but she has so many other qualities about her that make her an ideal mate for me.

We dated for about six months and I am so thankful to this website for making my dreams come true.

Take-Away: Always consider an upgrade on your next flight if offered. You'll find perks that you never knew existed in first class.

Twisted Sisters

I met a great girl on *Match.com* months ago. Her name is Melinda and she lived about 20 miles away from me in a town called Boca Raton, Florida. She was a personal assistant for a corporate executive and she lived in a condo by herself and her small dog. From the minute that we first dated, we clicked. I think we had instant chemistry. We liked the same foods, movies, etc. It really seemed like we found our soul mates. After dating a few weeks, the only thing that didn't progress as quickly as I would have liked was any real intimacy. I mean we kissed and hugged all the time, but we never consummated the relationship. She was worth the wait, I decided.

The following week, I asked Melinda to a concert at the casino, and she told me that her sister was coming into town, and that she wanted to check with her to make sure that her sister could make other plans for the night. I offered to buy another ticket for her sister, but she said that it shouldn't be a problem…"she has lots of friends here."

I picked Melinda up the following Friday night and she really looked super sexy. She was wearing a low cut blouse, very short skirt, and knee high boots. She really looked "hot" and I never saw her looking so sexy. As we drove to the casino, Melinda takes out from her purse an Altoid container, and instead of pulling out breath mints, she actually had rolled up joints in there. She asked me if I wanted her to light one up now, and I said "sure". I never even knew she smoked pot; although, I guess it never even came up in a conversation before, but we were going to a concert after all. So I took a couple of hits, as she did, and as much as I really liked Melinda prior to this date, I'm seeing a whole new side to her…a wild side. A side that was just icing on the cake.

We get to the venue, and Melinda grabs my hand and stays close to me. I instantly got the feeling that she's being very affectionate, probably due to the effect of the pot, but I didn't care why, as I enjoyed this side of her. We held hands during the concert, we smoked a couple more joints, and we drank a lot of beer. On the way home, Melinda fell asleep in the car, but practically had her head on my lap, which I also thought was very sexy and affectionate. When I got home, she asked me if I wanted to come in. Since I too was feeling a little buzzed, and it was late, I figured that although I probably wouldn't be getting any sex that night, it would still be nice to sleep with her.

We went into her place, and she told me to keep quiet as her sister was probably asleep in the bedroom. She turned the music on, kept the lights very dim, and we basically made out on the sofa. Melinda seemed very aggressive that night, which I didn't mind, and before I knew it, she practically ripped my clothes off me, as she instantly got on top of me.

We ended up making wild passionate love all night long. She was an animal. I mean, I don't know if it was the pot, the alcohol, or whatever, but it was the wildest sex I've had in a very long time. For someone who only hugged and kissed me prior to this night, I could swear I with someone else. Melinda was not only passionate but she seemed very experienced. She blew my mind.

I continued dating Melinda, but I've never had another night quite like that one. We've never smoked pot again, as she never brought it up, and although we've had sex often after that night, it was never that wild, and she never seemed like she knew what she was doing. Although I never met her sister that weekend, I did learn that she was a twin and oddly enough, her name was Belinda. Now maybe it's just me, but I often fantasized that maybe that it was Belinda I took to the concert that night, which definitely would have explained the total different personality of the girl I was with that evening. But no, it couldn't be. That would definitely be sick and twisted if that really did happen, and that only happens in fictional stories in adult magazines and not reality. But I'm telling you that the "concert girl" was not the same girl. I guess I'll never know the truth; however, her sister is coming back again for the holidays. I am going to find out exactly when, and I think I'll plan out another concert then. I just have to test out my theory because my imagination is really getting the best of me, and I just have a feeling that I'm going to have another crazy night once again when the sister comes to town.

Take-Away: *Remember when you couldn't wait for the circus to come to town when you were a kid? Some dreams never change. They just get better with age.*

Winning

We all know that many people don't like Charlie Sheen, but it hasn't always been that way. He only earned his somewhat despicable reputation in recent years. I actually met Charlie on the set of his show *Two and a half Men,* and I found him charming. Go Figure. Anyway, I had a day recently that made me feel like the winner Charlie used to be. He definitely was a dynamo in his day.

I have met several girls online who live in the Boca area, and three of them in particular were from three different dating sites. So, one Friday afternoon while I was staying at the Boca Marriott on business, I scheduled to meet one of them, Lauren. We were going to have lunch at the Brios Restaurant in the Boca Center right next to the Marriott. It was our first date and I was looking forward to seeing her in person. For a delightful change, she turned out not only to look like her profile pictures, but was much prettier as a matter of fact. There wasn't so much as a momentary lull in our conversation over lunch and the entire date was upbeat and exciting. We chatted about everything from past relationships to favorite foods. Three hours later we called it a day. I told her I would be calling her to get together again soon.

Meanwhile, I had made arrangements to meet another young lady at a Mexican restaurant in the same plaza at 5:30 p.m. I had actually had two prior dates with Suzanne while in town in the past, so we already knew each other fairly well. I knew her to be a spunky gal, and she was in prime form that evening. We quickly drank two pitchers of Margaritas while snacking on fresh guacamole and chips, and found ourselves not only buzzed from the Margaritas but buzzing our way right up to my hotel room where our two-person party only got better, if you get my drift. But by 8 o'clock, I pulled myself together and escorted Suzanne to her car and bid her goodnight. I told her I'd be looking forward to seeing her again next time I travelled to Boca. We kissed goodbye.

I had just enough time to trot back to my hotel room and freshen up before heading back out again. I had made dinner reservations at Morton's Restaurant located in the same hotel complex for 9:00 p.m. I was going to meet Gracie there. Gracie is a beautiful brunette who I met several years ago online and happens to be one of the sexiest ladies I've ever known. She arrived wearing a low cut, short black dress and looked like an absolute knock out. We had a delicious steak dinner, wine and shared a soufflé for dessert. I invited her back to my hotel for an after dinner drink and ended up in my room where our dinner date turned into an all-nighter.

Now I don't want to give the wrong impression here. I don't normally date three girls in one day much less sleep with two of them. But, heck, since I was flying back home the next afternoon, I really wanted to see both Gracie and Suzanne again while in Boca. Maybe crowding the lunch date in with Lauren put the whole thing over the top, but the good news is that I definitely want to see her again too. So what makes sense now is to book an extra day while I'm in Boca next time. That way I won't be so pressed to schedule all three of my Boca ladies into my itinerary. I'm sure Charlie would understand my strategy. He'd be the only one who would.

Take-Away: Sorry Charlie. There are many Players out there. Be careful. If you're looking for a true relationship, some sights are better than others.

Rules Are Meant To Be Broken

To be honest, my strategy for online dating always starts with the face, and then heads south from there. I'm a visually inclined guy, so before deciding to pursue or respond to a gal online she has to pass the "Looker" test with me. Now there are probably a lot of women out there who will think I am superficial, but I don't care. I just don't care! I've been dating for a long time and know what works for me. I've learned many things about women over the years and most of them, if asked, would say they had no negative remarks to make about their dating experience with me.

I recently met Lori online from a dating site. I decided to pursue her because her online photos passed my first test with flying colors.

We began messaging, texting and then talking by phone, which is the second strategy I use. I essentially complete an investigative interview to determine whether a girl is the type I would want to spend money on for a dinner date. The girls who make it to my second test think I'm simply having polite chit-chat with them in the beginning, but believe me I am very serious about the undercover work I'm doing in that phase of the dating process. The questions I ask probably seem completely innocuous, but believe me they reveal the things I want to know before I take step three, inviting the girl for a first date.

Lori's interviewing process actually went extremely well, and I determined she was worth springing for not only a dinner date, but an especially nice one at one of my favorite restaurants in the area. She accepted my invitation to *Abe and Louie's Steakhouse*

Our first dinner date was planned perfectly. Lori was punctual in arriving that Saturday night and looked pretty as her pictures. Over the course of our four hour meal, we had fun conversation and really enjoyed each other's company. I'd even have to say I enjoyed her more than my meal, a rarity in my world of first dates! There was one thing she said toward the end of our dinner that night though that really grabbed my attention. She said she was a very passionate person. Come on, you wouldn't expect a healthy guy to ignore that kind of comment as incidental, would you?

Then she added, "But, I live by the Seven Date Rule."

Well, I had never heard of the Seven Date Rule, so she had to explain it to me. She said it meant she would not get intimate with a guy until she went out with him for a minimum of seven times. She asked me if I could handle that. I said, "Of course! I'm in no rush." I kind of lied a little there, but I knew that was the answer she was looking for.

The following day was Sunday and it just so happened that the Delray Affair was going on, an annual event I love to attend. It is the most popular arts and crafts street festival in Palm Beach County, hosting hundreds of artists, craftsmen and photographers from all around the country. It is held outdoors along the palm tree lined streets of Atlantic Avenue, which they close off from vehicle traffic, making way for the hundreds of pedestrians who meander through the festival food vendors and strolling entertainers. I thought Lori might enjoy that sort of thing and I was right. We met up and spent the entire day together at the festival. It was really an enjoyable time.

Next afternoon I was thinking about her again and called to see if she was available for drinks after work that day. She said she would love to join me, and we met up at a local café on the water. We were just carrying on famously, bantering back and forth with what you might call kicks and giggles, when she said, "I know exactly what you're up to." "What are you talking about," I asked innocently enough?

She then said, "I know you have invited me out three days in a row so you can get laid by this coming weekend, huh?"

"What are you talking about?"

"Well, ever since I told you I have a Seven Date Rule, you seem to be pushing the calendar by inviting me out the next day. Are you thinking that four days in a row will get you into my pants quicker?"

I told her I had never thought such a thing…another little lie.

It turns out that we saw each other again the following Saturday night. It was only our fourth date together, but I was able to break her most important intimacy rule.

Take-Away: Ladies, many guys have one thing on their mind only. Stick to your guns. No sex without monogamy seems to be one rule. Don't feel pressure. A guy will wait for intimacy if he's really into you.

More Than A Grand Slam

When I first went to online dating I was very excited as I kept getting more and more messages from interested girls. Managing this stable of fillies was becoming a full time job, and I was burning the candle on both ends to keep up with my paying job and dating occupation. All this new-found female attention was thrilling, and I was going strong like the *Eveready* bunny, fully charged.

But as the weeks went by, I began to see a little problem developing. Since I lived in Connecticut and the girls I was attracting all lived in New York City, the hour and a half one-way commute was cutting in on my time that could otherwise be allocated to enlarging my stable. I was making that drive three or four times a week. Even though I had already met some great girls, I had absolutely no intention of limiting myself to anyone exclusively. I loved the variety, but knew in the longer run I was going to have to find a better way to keep up the pace of my exciting social life.

I came up with a genius idea. Instead of making the long drive to see one girl, I could schedule two girls on the same night to cut down the number of trips into the city. So I began starting earlier in the evening, meeting one girl at seven o'clock for dinner and another just for cocktails at 9:00. For a whole month this worked great, and I continued getting even more online messages from my dating site.

Then it occurred to me that if I took the train instead of driving I could manage dinner at seven, one quick cocktail at eight-thirty and a nightcap at 9:30, meeting three different lasses on the same night. I wouldn't have to worry about drinking and driving either. Why hadn't I thought of this great idea much sooner? So I pulled it off and was having a blast.

But listen to this. I came up with an even better idea, my ultimate plan. I realized that my dating life was costing me a fortune as I was then buying two dinners, two cocktails and two nightcaps every week seeing six women. I would be smarter to eliminate the dinners and just go for coffee or cocktails. As a matter of fact, my strategy then evolved to an even more brilliant plan of attack and my ultimate plan turned into a super-ultimate plan. By eliminating the lengthy and expensive dinner dates, I would have time and money to fit in an extra girl each night if I caught the five o'clock train. I could meet the first girl at six for coffee, next one at 7:15 for a drink, next at 8:30 and a nightcap with the fourth at 9:30. This super-ultimate plan worked, and for three weeks I kept it up.

I felt like the cock of the walk and brilliantly managing my growing flock of chicks!

Over two months on my terrific dating site had passed and I was still getting on average twenty new messages a day. I decided it was time to take drastic measures and devise the plot of all plots. Since I was spending a lot of money catching cabs and wasting time getting to the different venues for my four dates twice a week, I needed to eliminate the cab rides. Please try to understand my situation here. I was under a lot of pressure to keep up with so many requests to meet. I had no other choice but to go for more than a grand slam in the dating world. I decided to bat for five dates on the same night.

Here is how I did it. On one Thursday night I took the five o'clock train into the city and met my first date at Houstons. I planned on meeting her there at 6:15. I arranged for another girl to come at 7:15, one at 8:15, 9:15 and 10:15. They were all to meet me at the same place. I told each girl the same lie of a story on the phone prior to our meeting. I had plans with an old friend from college right after our date and that I wouldn't have much time to spend with them. So on the hour, I escorted each date out, told her how nice it was to meet her and continued strutting around the block before coming back to the same restaurant within fifteen minutes for my next appointment. Miraculously, it worked! But even more of a miracle was that I met the greatest girl on my last date at 10:15. I don't know whether or not she was actually the BEST one for me, but after all those drinks throughout the evening with the four prior dates, she looked the best to me. We ended up spending the night together back at her place and dating exclusively for a whole year…and she never found out about my exploits on that Thursday night…until now.

Take-Away: Some guys are real jerks. If you suspect that your date is seeing several women a night, or even several women a week, or even seven women a month…..run away as fast as you can. He's a player, or he thinks he is, and there are too many guys out there with good intentions that you don't need to settle. DON'T EVER SETTLE! Wait until you find "the one."

I Dream Of Jenny

Imagine the guy who goes on *Match.com* and comes across the profile of a woman who is looking for a man between the ages of thirty-five and forty-eight. Imagine that the picture shown is that of a really cute girl who comes with something a little extra…a baby on the way. How many guys would respond to the profile of a pregnant woman? My guess is not too many, but the ones who did got something they never imagined in a million years, a former Playboy playmate.

Jenny McCarthy, the sexy actress and playmate, admitted she's been using *Match.com* for dates. Although she's been accustomed to dating Hollywood hunks, NFL football players and even funnyman Jim Carey, she claims she has trouble meeting men in LA. She claims she's just looking for a normal guy.

"I don't care if they have a big nose. I don't care if they're bald. Just really sweet and (someone) who's a perfect reflection of who I am now…they have to have a job .I'd like them to be able to buy dinners and stuff like that. That is important."

So, believe it or not, McCarthy found her match, although not on an online site. She actually just married actor Donnie Wahlberg. Don't Despair. There are other rich and famous people on these dating sites that you would have never imagined. Yours truly met a hotel heiress on *Match*, and it's been rumored that Charley

Sheen's ex, Denise Richards, also had a profile up on a popular site. For those who think that the rich are only attracted to the rich or that the only way you will ever find a stunning beauty is by becoming a client of the Millionaire Matchmaker, you couldn't be more wrong. As a matter of fact, Patty Stanger, founder and CEO of Millionaire Matchmaker, didn't meet her fiancé at work. She met him on a free dating site called *Plenty of Fish!*

Take-Away: You never know who you might find with online dating. With over 40 million people who have explored this method of dating at one time or another, your appointment with Lady Luck could be today. You could hit the dating lottery and win your perfect mate, or get even luckier by winning the Powerball of internet dating, like a Jenny McCarthy. Either way, you can't win if you don't play. .

Kate Upton, Will You Go To The Prom With Me?

Talk about being the luckiest kid alive! Talk about using the internet to your fullest advantage! A Los Angeles teenager named Jake Davidson became an internet star when he posted a video called "Kate Upton, Will You Go To The Prom With Me?" His brilliant audio/visual invitation went viral with 2.6 million views and now Jake's life will forever be identified with the event.

Unfortunately, however, the famous "Sports Illustrated" swimsuit model was already booked on his milestone night and twittered him an extreme apology for being unable to accept. But, the blond bombshell's personal response to the young guy's fantasy date will no doubt be enough in itself to fuel his romantic imagination for years to come.

Then, as if the personal response from Upton wasn't thrilling enough, young Jake got yet another surprise as a result of the video's publicity. He captured the attention of Danish beauty Nina Agdal. Agdal, who like Upton has an impressive modeling resume, came forward and offered to be his prom date, and she's no second fiddle to Upton. This beauty made her modeling debut in the 2012 "Sports Illustrated" swimsuit issue and earned the title "Rookie of the Year." She also appeared in a Carl's Jr. television commercial that ran during the 2013 Super Bowl and was featured in a steamy photo spread in the May issue of "Esquire Magazine."

It is reported that Agdel, who is 21 years old, has now picked out her prom dress and is quoted as saying she is excited to meet her teenage beau. She will be wearing a sexy light colored gown with a daring slit back making Jake the envy of hundreds of guys who will be watching from the sidelines as he escorts his fantasy-come-true date to the prom.

Take-Away: Dreams do come true
There really is a God
Go Big or Go Home

Celebrity Online Daters

Like it or not, internet dating has always had a stigma attached to it. I've been getting dates through internet sites for years and people who know me still think I'm doing something creepy or just plain wrong. Even when I meet a lady through an online site, who I invite for a second or third date, she will inevitably say something like, "if our relationship moves to the next level, we'll have to tell our family and friends we met at work or at a party, OK?"

But, the good news is that the whole online dating thing is coming into its own. Celebrities who are successful, beautiful and available can now be found on certain dating sites, and in most cases not using aliases either. I heard recently that there were a couple of A and B listers who were on some popular sites, Hollywood celebrities like Jenny McCarthy and Martha Stewart. Something else I learned was that there are many celebrities who have tried online dating over the years, but no one knew about it then.

One confirmed online dater is the fabulously beautiful Halle Berry. Can you believe that? She has to be one of the sexiest Academy Award winning actresses in Hollywood. She has been quoted as saying, "I am never who I am. I have been to a couple of dating ones (sites) just to see what everybody is talking about." I love you, Halle, but come on! That's like a person saying they have no interest in the "swinging scene" but visits and signs up on swinger sites just to see what they're about. Really? OK, however you wish to justify your behavior Halle. No harm, no foul.

Another celebrity online dater is Mathew Perry, the actor from one of the most successful television franchises ever, "Friends". He has admitted to searching online for a significant other. And Deborah Ann Woll, the stunning and sexy actress from "True Blood", not only searched online for a beau, but found Mr. Perfect on *Match.com*. How about finding Grammy Award winner Adele's profile on an online dating site? She is quoted as saying, "I can't put a photo of myself, so I don't get any emails." Wow! As if that young lady would not already have enough suitors to pick from. And don't judge "Dancing With The Stars" Carrie Ann Inaba for looking for her significant other on *eHarmony*. She found him there and was even engaged to the guy for a period of time.

A real shocker, but the late comedian Joan Rivers herself was also a celebrity online dater. "I love smart men, funny men, elegant men," she stated in her profile.

To that, I say, "There is nothing sexier than a funny woman!" We're going to miss you Joan!

Think You're Too Good For Online Dating?

All you naysayers who believe that online dating is beneath you, listen up! Maybe it used to be true that online dating was the playground for people who were losers at face to face meetings at bars, their workplace, a party or social function, but not so today. It's now considered mainstream protocol in the dating world, and to prove my point, look who's doing it. She is America's social butterfly, cooking wizard, party planner, crafts aficionado and homemaker extraordinaire, the one and only Martha Stewart. Martha is the newest entrant into this billion dollar industry, and although she's been promoting her book in her online profile, I'll wager it's only a matter of time before we start seeing a new dating site called *Martha Stewart Millionaire Matchmaker Diva.com*.

On the dating site she's signed up on right now though, her profile name is "Thegoodlonglife", and she makes no bones about what she's looking for. She's scouting for a man between 55 and 70 who would be her ideal mate. She's even using her real picture, a sexy one too I might add. She says, "I was reminded how central good relationships are to happiness and longevity. Also I've always been a big believer that technology, if used well, can enhance one's life. So here I am, looking to enhance my dating life."

So what exactly is Martha looking for? She's looking for the same thing as everyone else, a true mate. She says, "Ideally, someone who's intelligent, established and curious, and who relishes adventure and new experiences as much as I do. Someone who can teach me new things. A lover of animals, grandchildren and the outdoors. Young at heart."

Most importantly, Martha is looking for someone who is not attracted to her for her fame and fortune. She honestly believes that her ideal partner is out there somewhere, and she is taking her search very seriously. She is receiving thousands of emails each week, so must rely on her assistants to comb through the lot to screen for only the best possible candidates.

Take-Away: Online dating sites are not only socially acceptable today, but perhaps fashionable as well. As you know, if Martha Stewart is doing it, it must be good because everything she touches seems to turn to gold......except maybe stocks.

Lobster Love

This girl and guy met online, and they eventually agree on a dinner date to meet personally after weeks of internet chat. Theirs had been a no-pressure, let's take our time getting know each other-type of internet socializing. It proved to be a good foundation for their relationship.

"What's your favorite food?" he asks.

With no equivocation she replies, "Lobster!" "Where do you get lobster in your town?" he asks.

"Red Lobster, my favorite, favorite, favorite!" she asserts. "Red Lobster? Do they even sell lobsters there?" he questions.

Tickled with excitement over both her playful online beau and a Red Lobster dinner in the making, the girl giggles, "Of course they do, silly."

"No. No. I mean do they sell REAL lobsters...LIVE lobsters?"

"Yes. Oh, yes. They even have a big lobster tank right there at the front door when you walk in," she ever-so-proudly assures him, and they then finalize scheduling the day and time for their first date, meeting at the Red Lobster in the girl's hometown, 7 p.m. Sunday evening.

"I'll tell you what, my dear, if we continue to date I will take you to MY favorite place for lobster someday, okay?"

"Can't wait!"

Their first date was a beautiful success and after four more weeks of dating, they began considering themselves to be an exclusive couple. Anyone who knew the twosome could see there was a spark of heart and soul growing between them, the kind of spark that can potentially ignite a life-long relationship in matrimony. But for them, no quantum leap of matrimonial commitment was needed to keep either one satisfied. They were simply enjoying the slow and steady pace of their budding romance.

Then one Sunday afternoon the guy picks her up for their date, but refuses to tell where they are going. He drives to the airport and parks at a small terminal. She's surprised and excited over what is suddenly becoming a mysterious adventure-date, but even more so when he leads her up the steps of a small, private luxury jet. Inside the aircraft, she is enthralled with the custom leather upholstery and hand-crafted, wood detail. The jet was top of the line air transportation, and shortly after takeoff the stewardess served the couple champagne in fine stemware. It was only a short time later when they landed in Portland, Maine where a private limousine was waiting to chauffeur them into town.

Their afternoon was a shopping extravaganza in Freeport. From LL Bean to Polo to Coach, she was lavished with more gifts than could barely fit with them into the limo. This prince of a guy couldn't have given his princess a more wonderful day.

But…he had one more surprise. Just as the sun was setting at precisely 7 p.m., the limo delivered them to the front doors of Mabel's Restaurant, home of the freshest lobster in the country.

The girl never went to a Red Lobster again the rest of her life.

__Take-Away:__ Never set your expectations too high. You'll only be in for a major disappointment. You'll appreciate your date much more when you don't expect much, and they surprise you beyond your wildest dreams.

Take Me Out With The Crowd

I've been on *Match.com* for many years, and since I've lived in both New York and Florida have had the opportunity to take dates to a wide variety of sporting events. You see sports are a big part of my life, as is dating, and I've learned something valuable about their connection to each other in the getting-to-know-you world of first dates. Taking a first date to a spectator sport can clarify three very important things right off the bat.

First, you will find out if your date is a good sport by the way she deals with the crowds, hecklers and chaos that goes on at sporting events. You'll see whether she is patient when the parking lot is crammed and lines are long. You'll discover her ability to be flexible when the game goes eighteen innings instead of nine, and how much stamina she has when it's thirty-two degrees in the bleachers and snowing.

Second, there is no awkwardness in the conversation on a first date at a sports event because in a crowd of boisterous fans feverishly rooting for their team you can choose to talk or not. It won't matter. If she is a non-stop rambler, doesn't matter. If she says nothing, doesn't matter. Either way, the noise all around makes it completely acceptable to keep a primary focus on the game and conversation secondary. This can be a very telling factor to observe on a first date and can be a deal-breaker for many guys.

Then thirdly, taking a first time date to a sporting event will show you a lot about her eating habits. You will quickly see whether she is a health freak, a vegetarian or just one of the guys and willing to eat hotdogs, drink beer and pig out on nachos and popcorn.

Yes, these three insights are helpful in the dating world. Pay attention to the wisdom of my years on this and you won't make many "second" date mistakes.

It was my first date with Sheila. I picked her up to take her to a baseball game. She had packed a picnic lunch for us, which I thought was very sweet and an unexpected gesture on her part. We got to the park and saw that bags were being checked at the entrance so I helped Sheila stash most of the food items in our jackets to smuggle in. Unfortunately we had to abandon some cans of soda and a nice bottle of wine, but no big deal. We took our seats in my company's box which is behind first base. The die-hard season ticket holders were already there and settled into their seats all around us. The guys acknowledged our arrival and a couple of them gave me a wink, which let me know they could see Sheila didn't fit the mold of my usual date. First, Sheila was a bit older than most and second, she had a classy style. Luckily, the guys left me alone without any heckling because they could tell I was trying to be on my best behavior. I appreciated that.

As my seatmates were stuffing their sloppy faces with hotdogs, cheese nachos, pretzels with mustard, and beer, Sheila then started to prepare our little feast. First she spread out a little blanket over our laps followed by her really impressive picnic snacks. There were whole wheat crackers with humus, brie, fresh burrata, spinach and artichoke dip, guacamole and fresh strawberries. I was impressed, but my fellow fans with the nacho cheese dripping off their chins found good cheer in starting to poke jokes about our snacks.

"Monsieur! Garcon!" they started yelling with an uppity French accent, "Merci! Merci beaucoup! Si' l vous plait?" Our hostess ignored them completely.

As a matter of fact their fancy French act became so animated and loud that everyone around our box was watching us instead of the game! With every new item Sheila pulled out for us to eat, their jolly humor rose to an even higher pitch. I will admit, they were making some pretty funny jokes, and I think Sheila was just a little embarrassed over it all. There she was trying to feed me her impressive gourmet food and at the same time had to endure insulting remarks from the peanut gallery around us.

We laughed about it all afterwards. I told her the picnic was really the nicest thing any date had ever done for me. She knew I appreciated her efforts, and her feelings weren't hurt at all. We had many more dates after that one, and I guarantee you they were all much more romantic than that one. She had come through our first date in good form.

Take-Away: *You can learn a lot about a person by taking them out of their "comfort zone".*

A Real Catch

I met a great girl on *Match.com*. Her name is Amy. From the beginning, she appeared to engender everything I was looking for in a partner. She was attractive, educated and loved sports. From my viewpoint that's what I call the total package.

We scheduled our first date for dinner at a very casual restaurant in the City. Amy was so easy to talk to and the time flew by that evening as we got to know each other better. We talked about so many different topics that interested both of us, but then I mentioned I was going to the Yankee game the following day and her eyes really lit up. When I saw such a reaction from her, I immediately invited her to join me. She was thrilled. And since I had a box and an extra ticket, I felt like the stars were lining up in my favor for an amazing weekend with my special new lady.

I hired a car service to pick Amy up at 11 a.m. next morning at her apartment and then deliver us to Yankee Stadium. Under normal circumstances, I'd have taken the train, but on this day I wanted to class it up just a bit to impress her. She was ready and waiting in the lobby of her complex when the limo arrived and looked cute as anything dressed in her short skirt, sexy little top and wearing a Yankee baseball cap. Our driver muscled his way through traffic and delivered us to the stadium in no time at all where we quickly joined in the buzz of excitement.

There were several other guys from my company already seated in our box on the first base line. I introduced my darling date and got the nod from all of them that they approved of my companion. Amy did look hot! She was completely unpretentious and quickly joined the lot of us drinking beer and rooting wildly for the home team. She even ate a hotdog smothered with chili and cheese and made a bit of a sloppy mess of it, which made her even more genuine to be with.

Then in the seventh inning Alex Rodriguez, who happened to be Amy's favorite player, hit a line drive just several rows in front of us. A fan tried to catch it on the fly, but it ricocheted off his hand and was knocked down, spiraling under the seat in front of us. Everyone around there dove for the gold, including me. It was a mass of hands, arms and bodies in the scramble, but somehow I came up with the ball. I couldn't believe my luck! I'd been faithfully going to games for five years and never before came close to snagging one, much less one that came off the bat of Alex Rodriguez. I was hailed as royalty when I waived the ball in the air to let everyone in the stands see who got the prize.

Now here is where I actually surprised myself. As much as I wanted that ball as a keepsake, I was overtaken by Amy's beauty, smiling face and the fact that Alex Rodriguez was her favorite player. Without hesitation I handed it over to her.

"No. I couldn't," she insisted.

But I insisted more that she hold onto it forever, and never forget that she got it while on the best date of her life. With that, she promised she would always remember me, and said she couldn't have been happier if she'd won the lottery. I promise you, it was one of the best dates I ever had.

I dated Amy for about a year after that. We're still the best of friends. *She still has my ball.*

Pretty Woman

As a young woman I often had the dream of being swept off my feet by a gorgeous guy and having a fairy tale ending. What woman hasn't? So when I saw the movie "Pretty Woman" I decided I would imitate Julia Roberts' character and look for my own Edward Lewis. It was then that I discovered the dating website called *Seeking Arrangement's*. Its platform features sugar daddy gentlemen who are willing to help someone like me in exchange for friendship and companionship. The help I needed at that point was support to finish school. It was on that website that I found both help and my Prince Edward.

His name is Charles. My first meeting with him was at the Capitol Grille. We had an amazing dinner, amazing conversation and there was instant chemistry between the two of us. We met for dinner on two more occasions and each time Charles sent me flowers the following day. His attached handwritten cards read, "Each time I see you, it gets better and better. Thanks for making me happy again. Charles."

On our next date Charles told me he was going to be out of the country for a couple of weeks on business. He asked if I had a passport. I did. He then asked if I would consider meeting him in Paris and I didn't hesitate for a moment to accept the invitation. He was delighted. When I told him I'd never been there, he responded with a dignified bow saying, "Madame, I am your personal tour guide to the City of Lovers." I couldn't wait to go.

Charles' office sent me my plane ticket the following week. It was first class seating. Since I had never flown first class anywhere in my life, much less to Paris, you can imagine how thrilled I was. I anxiously counted down the hours over the following week until I boarded my flight to France.

When I arrived, there was a car waiting for me. The driver literally whisked me off to my hotel, and what a hotel it was! It was a Four Seasons Hotel called George V and absolutely the most decadent, beautiful place I'd ever seen. There were fountains and statutes everywhere accented with huge arrangements of fresh cut flowers. The lobby had high ceilings that were covered with ornate gold molding. There were expansive paned windows draped with heavy tapestries and the floors were polished marble. The furnishings were magnificent. Every detail screamed, "Rich. Rich. Rich."

I checked in and was told Charles would be arriving later in the afternoon. The concierge introduced himself, welcoming me warmly and insisting his service was at my beck and call. He even offered one of his assistants to escort me during the afternoon to the Champs-Elysees one block away should I wish to go shopping before Charles arrived. I thanked him and was then shown to my room. It wasn't a room though; it was a suite that was as big as my house. Iced champagne in silver was carted in by a butler and by now I knew this trip was simply going to be over the top! I opted to drench myself in a luxurious bath and prepare for my Prince to arrive.

When Charles came through the door several hours later, I was relaxed and so happy. We embraced like lovers in a romance novel. "Are the accommodations acceptable?" he asked with a smile, and I told him I wouldn't mind at all roughing it with him for a few days.

Charles suggested that we go out for the afternoon because we had lots of things to do and see. The first stop was a famous shopping area where there were stores of every famous international designer known. There were outdoor cafes and theaters. It was spectacular. As we leisurely strolled along the streets of Paris, Charles told me I was going to need a dress for dinner that evening. I told him I had brought one, but he insisted that I should have something new to wear in a new city. He led me into a famous boutique and an hour later, I had an amazing low back dress, fabulous shoes and matching designer handbag. I felt so adored and expressed my heartfelt feelings openly to Charles. His reply was simply, "A beautiful outfit for a beautiful woman." Charles has a way with words.

I, on the other hand, am struggling to find the vocabulary to describe all the details of my three days in Paris. You'll just have to imagine for yourself when I say it was the best time of my life. Our dinner that first night couldn't have been more romantic as we sat by candlelight with a view of the Seine River. The next day we visited the Eiffel Tower and had the most romantic dinner there at one of the most famous restaurants in the world. The views of the City from up there were incredible and left me with memories most people can only read about in a book. I will never ever forget that experience for as long as I live!

We spent the next day sightseeing and shopping. I couldn't get enough of both. We went to the Louvre where I saw the famous painting of Mona Lisa and visited Notre Dame Cathedral, the Arc de Triumph and many other historic places. We even had lunch while cruising the River Seine. It was all so romantic and a girl's fairy tale come true. Charles made me feel so special and so loved that I still can't believe I met this man online. I felt like the luckiest girl in the world and wished that the trip would never end.

It's been almost six months now since leaving Paris and I am truly in love with Charles, and he with me. He seems so appreciative being with me and I feel the same. I'd be surprised if marriage isn't in the near future for us. If he asks, I will say, "Yes!" I want to spend the rest of my life with him and live this fairy tale to the end of time with my real life Prince Charles.

Take-Away: It's true, you have to kiss a lot of frogs before you find your prince or princess. But when you do, you'll realize that it was well worth the wait.

Don't Marry For Money

I think way too much is made of the income question on dating website profiles. Most women I know look at the answer to that question right after they find an attractive guy. The problem for us gals is that probably 99% of the time the information is inaccurate. The truth is that most guys inflate their income so that they can find a woman who is, more often than not, young and attractive and easily influenced by rich men. Very rarely will you find a guy who answers the question about income truthfully. It's even rarer to find a man who deflates his income, but I found one.

Ted's profile picture appealed to me. I found him on one of the more popular dating sites, and I would be lying if I said I didn't look at his income. I did. He had checked the box that showed his income to be between $25K and $50K, and since he was a teacher that income bracket made sense. I shot an email off to him and he replied.

I told my girlfriend about him and she said I shouldn't go out with him. "You need someone who can support you," she insisted. "Why are you wasting your time on a loser like that? There are so many men online that make loads of money."

I ignored her advice and after Ted and I emailed back and forth several more times, we lined up a meeting to have drinks after work. From the moment I saw him in person, I knew he was special. He was very attractive and I felt instant chemistry. I had the feeling he felt the same about me. It wasn't long after our first date that we agreed to be in a monogamous relationship.

Ted lived on the east end, off First Avenue in a nice one bedroom with great views of Roosevelt Island. In that location, I knew his place had to be super expensive, and I wondered how he could afford it on a teacher's salary. I never brought it up of course, but after meeting his mother and seeing that she was very classy and well dressed, I figured she was probably subsidizing him. None of that money stuff mattered to me though. I had fallen in love with the person, Ted.

It's been two years now since Ted and I first met, and I have a four carat diamond engagement ring on my finger. It turns out that Ted comes from a prominent family and has a trust account that will give us financial security for the rest of our lives. I feel like I'm the luckiest girl in the world! I'm so glad that I didn't listen to my girlfriend's advice in the beginning or I'd have never met the man of my dreams.

Take-Away: Don't marry for money because fortunes can come and go. Marry for love and always stand by your man. If it's true love from the beginning, it will work.

Here's To You Mrs. Robinson

You've heard the expression "You have to kiss a lot of frogs to find a prince", right? Usually the line is used by women, but it ought to be used in my case as a guy to say "I've had to kiss a lot of frogs to find my princess!" I've actually found two princesses along my way.

The first one was someone who was much older than me. I was twenty years her junior, and when that romance began she said she felt like Mrs. Robinson. The first time I heard her make the reference to herself I asked, "Who's Mrs. Robinson?" I was just kidding of course, but I'm sure it made her wonder whether I was really was too young to remember the classic movie, "The Graduate" starring the young Dustin Hoffman.

From the moment I saw Sheila I was smitten. She was elegant, classy, sophisticated, worldly, funny, charming and warm hearted. She drove an older vintage Mercedes and was a writer for a small town publication. And did I say, Sheila was a real looker. She was a tall, long legged brunette.

I dated her for about a month before I really came to know her. She had several children who were all older and living away from home. A year earlier she had divorced her compulsively controlling husband who was the father of her children and brought to an end their twenty-two year marriage. She told me she lived in a very private neighborhood with hardly any neighbors around. I had never seen her home, but she promised to show it to me one day soon.

One night after going to the movies together, Sheila thought it would be a good time to show me where she lived. It was a palace. The place was an estate of more than two hundred acres and a home with twenty thousand square feet, not to mention a six-car garage with central heat and air, indoor pool and tennis court. I was in disbelief. It was the most impressive home I had ever seen and since I worked in the luxury real estate business, I fancied myself to think I had seen the best of them all. I hadn't until then. Sheila was heir to a hotel fortune. The relationship I had with this princess lasted for over a year.

Take-Away: You never know who you will meet in your travels, and you never know who you will meet online. You have now heard plenty of the disaster stories, bad dating experiences and misrepresentation problems with online dating, but it only takes finding one good one along the way to make the dating efforts worthwhile. Heck, I've had the good fortune of finding several.

My second princess was Tracy. When we first met she had a great job with a travel publication and we were together for many years. During our relationship she started her own luxury travel business and ultimately became one of the leading travel agents in the country. During our time together we traveled the globe. We've been everywhere from Barcelona to Cork Ireland, from Rome to Lisbon, Monte Carlo to the Greek Isles. Honestly, there are a few places we didn't explore together. My favorite, if I had to choose one, was our trip to South Africa; where we explored the beauty of Capetown, the amazing wine vineyards and of course we went on several of the finest safaris in the world.

Take-Away: If it hadn't been for Tracy, who opened my eyes to places I never imagined visiting, my life would not be as enriched as it is today. I'm grateful that Tracy actually found me, nearly ten years ago, and we had the opportunity to travel the world together...thanks to online dating.

A Match Made In Heaven

I came across an amazing girl on a popular matchmaking site, and I must say that although I've always been a skeptic about finding my ideal girl online, I may have hit the jackpot with Meghan. In her profile, she wrote exactly what she was looking for in a guy. It read: *Just looking for an easy non-committal relationship for now that could lead to more in the future. I just came out of a long term union with a great guy. We were together for two years, and it actually took me that long to realize that I couldn't see a future with him. It was painful to say goodbye, but I knew it was best for both.* Meghan continued to say that she was looking for no drama, no stress, no kids, no baggage and furthermore that she just wanted to have fun, great dinners, lots of laughs, spontaneous romantic travel, amazing sex with a guy who is not full of himself, one who is a good dresser, sarcastic humor, lots of hair and hasn't lied too much on his profile. She ended the narrative with, "Is that asking too much?"

I loved it! I could tell she was exactly who I'd been searching for. She was smart, witty, pretty and seemed to be down to earth and not a gold digger on any level. I couldn't wait to meet her. She lived in the Sunny Isles area of Florida, which is in North Miami Beach, so not too far from where I lived and making our possible new relationship workable from a logistical standpoint. Were the stars aligning just right for me?

I met Meghan for dinner on a Saturday night and she was just as attractive as her profile pictures showed her to be, and even sexier in person. During our meal she explained that she had just recently moved down to Miami after ending a long term relationship. She was in the process of finding employment, but said she wasn't too worried about landing a job since she had a very strong academic background. She had been a school teacher for many years and felt she could always go back to that profession if nothing more interesting came along. She was presently living with a friend. She told me she didn't have a car but was optimistic about getting her own place and vehicle as soon as she became employed. She was adamant that she had no intention of allowing a guy to financially support her since she had "been there, done that" and learned her lesson.

After several more dates with Meghan, I began to really fall for her. She was not only a great gal but was a great match for me. She was proving to be exactly what I'd been looking for in a woman, and it didn't take long before I invited her to move in with me. That was six months ago and to date, our relationship has been the most compatible and stress-free of any I've ever experienced. We don't fight at all. There's no drama. She has since taken a good teaching job and bought a car for herself. We just couldn't be happier. We keep discovering more and more how well we are matched as a couple, and have even begun planning a long vacation together in Italy.

Although it's only been a few months, I can't imagine my life without Meghan. I think she feels the same way about me. If it wasn't for *Match*, I would have never found the potential love of my life. I'll keep you posted.

Epilogue

Haven't Met You Yet

I've been on over five hundred dates in the past fifteen years, and just like the Michael Buble song "Haven't Met You Yet", I'm still searching for my "one and only". I do feel that I'm now extremely closer than ever before, and I'm very optimistic that I will find her someday.

It's everyone's dream of finding a relationship and love. If this weren't true, why would there be so many online dating sites with more popping up all the time? With new sites coming online every day, and dating apps like *Tinder* now becoming the norm, the number of singles using or having used online dating is fast approaching 50,000,000. But with all these sites and all the information in the profiles, there has never once been a perfect match on paper. It doesn't matter either how much you pay for a dating service, whether online or off, because the perfect match involves a highly complex human equation.

Even Patty Stanger's service and television series "Million Dollar Matchmaker" can't guarantee a match. If you pay the minimum fee of $10,000, the best you can expect is opportunity. Patty herself had to expand her own opportunities for a relationship and ultimately found her guy on a free online service that was not in any way associated with her company or television series.

Epilogue

I think the reason these online services can never promise a successful union is because just like my profession of real estate, matchmaking is not an exact science. There's simply no way of predicting whether or not two will have chemistry until they meet face to face. No online photo, video, Facebook or otherwise techno avenues will guarantee success. Face to face with a real, live person is the only way to determine whether there is a meeting of the minds or meeting of the looks. What is attractive to one person may not be attractive to another. Yes, human relationships and love involve a complex equation full of surprise and mystery.

So, as I continue to travel the country to find the right woman, I continue to believe in love. Whether I find my true love online or on a plane doesn't matter because as in Buble's lyrics, I give so much more than I get, and I know that when I least expect it I will find the love of my life. After all, Buble finally did. And my parents are still holding hands after 61 years.

Take-Away: *If matching profiles really worked, then the phrase "opposites attract" would have no relevance.*

There is hope for us all.

Author's Story

Donald Gorbach started research for this book almost fifteen years ago. At that time, he had no idea his active dating life would result in a collection of stories more amazing than Ripley's "Believe It Or Not." From models and actresses to celebrities and multi-millionaires, he has wined, dined and danced them all! His dates with professional escorts, a beauty queen, several porn queens, a dominatrix or two, and even women who were once men, are among some of the spicier personal stories he shares in this book.

Although he has been telling his internet dating stories for years, and collecting them from other singles across the country, this is his first time entertaining listeners in literary form with his favorites. The whole of these dating adventure stories will leave you with images of some of the nicest, kindest, funniest and most interesting people imaginable. All of their identities must remain anonymous, but their quest is no secret. They are all hoping to find companionship and that special someone to love.

Donald is a graduate of Vanderbilt University and along with his passion for writing, he is a Real Estate Broker in Palm Beach, Florida. He is the author of *101 Greatest Real Estate Stories Ever Told, Ready, Willing & Unbelievable*, and has several other "reality storybooks" in development.